THE OFFICIAL
ULTIMATE
80s
POP QUIZ

THE OFFICIAL ULTIMATE 80s POP QUIZ

Virgin
BOOKS

Published by Virgin Books 2009

2 4 6 8 10 9 7 5 3 1

Based on quiz questions compiled by
Dave McAleer, Matt White and Phil Matcham

First published in Great Britain in 2009 by Virgin Books
Random House, 20 Vauxhall Bridge Road, London SW1V 2SA

www.virginbooks.com
www.rbooks.co.uk

Addresses for companies within The Random House Group Limited can be found
at: www.randomhouse.co.uk/offices.htm

The Random House Group Limited Reg. No. 954009

A CIP catalogue record for this book
is available from the British Library

ISBN 9780753516911

The Random House Group Limited supports The Forest Stewardship Council (FSC),
the leading international forest certification organisation. All our titles that are
printed on Greenpeace-approved FSC certified paper carry the FSC logo.

Our paper procurement policy can be found at www.rbooks.co.uk/environment

FSC

Printed in the UK by CPI Bookmarque, Croydon, CR0 4TD

CONTENTS

THE OFFICIAL ULTIMATE 80s POP QUIZ

GUESS THE SONG

1. **What was the title of Spandau Ballet's one and only No. 1 single?**

   a. 'Through The Barricades' *b.* 'Gold' *c.* 'True'

2. **Which country appeared in the title of Kim Wilde's No. 12 hit from 1981?**

   a. 'Switzerland' *b.* 'Cambodia' *c.* 'China'

3. **Which South African township did Malcolm McLaren sing about in his 1983 hit?**

   a. 'Sharpeville' *b.* 'Sun City' *c.* 'Soweto'

4. **Which of the following was *not* a No. 1 for John Lennon in 1981?**

   a. 'Nobody Told Me' *b.* 'Imagine' *c.* 'Woman'

5. **What was Stephen 'Tin Tin' Duffy's final chart entry in 1985?**

   a. 'Icing On The Cake' *b.* 'Fruit Cake'

   c. 'Have Your Cake And Leave'

6. **What was the title of Sting's debut solo single of 1982?**

   a. 'Try A Little Tenderness' *b.* 'Kindness'

   c. 'Spread A Little Happiness'

7. **Who was Ian Dury 'profoundly in love with' in the mid-'80s?**

   a. Pandora *b.* Profanity *c.* Paula

For answers see p267

8. In 1981, Altered Images and Stevie Wonder both had No. 2 hits with songs with which same title?

a. 'I Just Called To Say I Love You'

b. 'Happy Birthday'   *c.* 'Go Wild In The Country'

9. Which 1983 Rolling Stones video was banned?

a. 'She Was Hot'   *b.* 'Undercover Of The Night'

c. 'Start Me Up'

10. When Texas made their chart debut in 1989, what did they not want?

a. A Lover   *b.* A Brother-In-Law   *c.* A Toyboy

For answers see p267

NO. 1 SINGLES

1. **Which school choir had a No. 1 with 'There's No One Quite Like Grandma'?**

   a. St Paul's   *b.* St Francis's   *c.* St Winifred's

2. **Who did Phil Collins duet with on 'Easy Lover'?**

   a. Michael Jackson   *b.* Lionel Richie   *c.* Philip Bailey

3. **The Police's 'Every Breath You Take' was later used as the basis for which rap chart-topper?**

   a. 'Ice Ice Baby' – Vanilla Ice   *b.* 'Stan' – Eminem

   c. 'I'll Be Missing You' – Puff Daddy

4. **In 1986, George Michael had a different what?**

   a. Girlfriend   *b.* Boyfriend   *c.* Corner

5. **Who was travelling 'All Around The World' in 1989?**

   a. Lisa Stansfield   *b.* Tracy Chapman   *c.* Gloria Estefan

6. **'Do They Know It's Christmas?' was a No. 1 in 1989 by which act?**

   a. Band Aid   *b.* Band Aid II   *c.* Band Aid III

7. **Which chart-topper was previously recorded as a B-side by Tina Turner?**

   a. 'The Only Way Is Up' – Yazz & The Plastic Population

   b. 'Ride On Time' – Black Box

   c. 'Don't Turn Around' – Aswad

For answers see p267

8. **Name Simple Minds' only No. 1.**

    a. 'Don't You (Forget About Me)'

    b. 'Belfast Child'   *c.* 'Alive And Kicking'

9. **Ray Dorset, the leader of Mungo Jerry, wrote which No. 1?**

    a. 'Pass The Dutchie' – Musical Youth

    b. 'Feels Like I'm In Love' – Kelly Marie

    c. 'Every Loser Wins' – Nick Berry

10. **In 1989, what did Black Box do on time?**

    a. Arrive   *b.* Appear   *c.* Ride

For answers see p267

ROCK ALBUMS

1. **Released in 1988, what was the title of Magnum's most successful album?**

   a. Wings Of Heaven   *b.* Marauder   *c.* The Eleventh Hour

2. **Complete this album title: _____ At The Lost And Found.**

   a. Midday   *b.* 11.53 p.m.   *c.* Midnight

3. **Who puckered up for *Barbed Wire Kisses* in 1988?**

   a. Inspiral Carpets   *b.* The Cure

   c. The Jesus & Mary Chain

4. **Which 'Smooth' rocker rode on *The Swing Of Delight* in 1980?**

   a. John Mellencamp   *b.* Tom Petty   *c.* Carlos Santana

5. **Name Jim Steinman's only charting album.**

   a. Back For Good   *b.* Bad For Good

   c. Rock 'N' Roll For Good

6. **What was Whitesnake's 1981 album called?**

   a. Come And Get It

   b. Go And Never Come Back

   c. Coming And Going

7. **Clean-shaven drummer Frank Beard contributed to which of these albums?**

   a. Eliminator   *b.* Full Moon Fever   *c.* Dead Ringer

For answers see p267

8. **Which Californian band formed in 1984 but did not have a UK chart smash until 1995?**

   a. Smashing Pumpkins   *b.* Pearl Jam   *c.* The Offspring

9. **How hot were Bon Jovi in 1985?**

   a. 7800 Fahrenheit   *b.* At Boiling Point   *c.* 3900 Centigrade

10. **Which band featuring Midge Ure released *The Anvil*?**

    a. Extended Period Of Leave   *b.* Visage   *c.* Ultravox

For answers see p267

POWER BALLADS

1. **Which band belted out the 1987 chart-topper 'Nothing's Gonna Stop Us Now'?**

    a. Jefferson Airplane   *b.* Starship   *c.* Jefferson Starship

2. **Name Laura Branigan's Top 10 hit from 1984.**

    a. 'The Unlucky One'   *b.* 'Hallelujah'   *c.* 'Self Control'

3. **Chicago's Peter Cetera was celebrating the glory of what in 1986?**

    a. Life   *b.* Love   *c.* Heartbreak

4. **He was a member of The Babys and Broken English and he was 'Missing You' in 1984? Who is he?**

    a. Jim Diamond   *b.* Mike Rutherford   *c.* John Waite

5. **Which one-hit wonder charted for 'The First Time' in 1988?**

    a. Robin Beck   *b.* Cara Tivey   *c.* Tiffany Darwish

6. **Name the song inspired by singer Mike Rutherford's relationship with his late father.**

    a. 'The Living Years'   *b.* 'Kayleigh'   *c.* 'Hard To Say I'm Sorry'

7. **Who, in late 1984, was the first of these three acts to chart with a song called 'The Power Of Love'?**

    a. Frankie Goes To Hollywood   *b.* Jennifer Rush

    c. Huey Lewis & The News

8. **When did Phil Collins make his chart debut with 'In The Air Tonight'?**

    a. 1981   *b.* 1983   *c.* 1985

For answers see p268

9. **Name the rock band whose hits include 'Hard To Say I'm Sorry' and 'Hard Habit To Break'.**

a. Styx   *b.* Chicago   *c.* Firehouse

10. **The album *Whitesnake 1987* spawned which power ballad classic?**

a. 'Broken Wings'   *b.* 'Is This Love'

c. 'I Should Have Known Better'

For answers see p268

COMPLETE THE NAME OF THE ACT

1. **Kid Creole & The** _____

2. **Derek** _____

3. **Atlantic** _____

4. _____ **City**

5. **The** _____ **Corporation**

6. **The Blow** _____

7. **Doug E. Fresh &** _____

8. **Hot** _____

9. **Aztec** _____

10. _____ **Romance**

Monkeys Chocolate Camera Far

Modern Coconuts Starr Inner

& The Dominos The Get Fresh Crew

For answers see p268

 **1980**

1. **Which of the following was a number one for Blondie in 1980?**

   a. 'Heart Of Glass'   *b.* 'Call Me'   *c.* 'Maria'

2. **In 1980, with whom did Cliff Richard share the vocals on the song 'Suddenly'?**

   a. Olivia Newton-John   *b.* Billy Ocean   *c.* Lulu

3. **Which act had its last Top 20 hit with 'Banana Republic'?**

   a. Slade   *b.* The Stranglers   *c.* The Boomtown Rats

4. **What was Sheena Easton's first Top 20 hit called?**

   a. 'Modern Girl'   *b.* 'One Man Woman'   *c.* '9 To 5'

5. **Complete the title of this 1980 Captain & Tennille hit: 'Do That To Me _____'.**

   a. Again   *b.* In The Morning   *c.* One More Time

For answers see p268

6. Name '80s chart regulars UB40's first hit?

    a. 'My Way Of Thinking' / 'I Think It's Going To Rain'

    b. 'The Earth Dies Screaming' / 'I Dream A Lie'

    c. 'King' / 'Food For Thought'

7. Who was '80s hit-maker Syreeta once married to?

    a. Billy Preston   *b.* Marvin Gaye   *c.* Stevie Wonder

8. 'And The Beat Goes On' was the biggest hit by which group?

    a. Ottawan   *b.* The Whispers   *c.* Lipps Inc

9. What was the only hit by Fiddler's Dram?

    a. 'Turning Japanese'

    b. 'There's No One Quite Like Grandma'

    c. 'Daytrip To Bangor (Didn't We Have A Lovely Time)'

10. Who was 'A Fool For Your Loving'?

    a. Chris Rea   *b.* Elkie Brooks   *c.* Whitesnake

For answers see p268

◎ COMPLETE THE NAME OF THE ACT

1. _____ In A Box

2. Bow Wow _____

3. Deacon _____

4. Jack 'N' _____

5. Cutting _____

6. Huey Lewis & The _____

7. _____ Factory

8. Third _____

9. _____ & The Sunshine Band

10. The Matchroom _____

News   KC   Fiction   World

Mob   Living   Blue   Wow

Chill   Crew

For answers see p269

MATCH THE TOP 10 GROUP AND THEIR SINGER

1. Slade

2. The Style Council

3. Swing Out Sister

4. Van Halen

5. Styx

6. The Stone Roses

7. The Teardrop Explodes

8. Soft Cell

9. Tenpole Tudor

10. Toto

Julian Cope   Eddie Tenpole

David Lee Roth   Marc Almond   Corinne Drewery

Bobby Kimball   Dennis DeYoung   Noddy Holder

Paul Weller   Ian Brown

For answers see p269

 **SIMPLY RED**

1. **Name Simply Red's least successful chart single (No. 68 in 1988)?**

   a. 'I Won't Feel Bad'   b. 'You've Got It'   c. 'It's Only Love'

2. **When was Mick Hucknall born?**

   a. 8 June 1950   b. 8 June 1960   c. 8 June 1970

3. **What was Simply Red's debut Top 20 single in 1985?**

   a. 'Come To My Aid'

   b. 'Money's Too Tight (To Mention)'

   c. 'Jericho'

4. **'Holding Back The Years' peaked at which number in November 1985?**

   a. No. 51   b. No. 2   c. No. 29

5. **Simply Red were named after Mick Hucknall's what?**

   a. Hair colour

   b. Allegiance to Manchester United Football Club

   c. Love of the Labour Party

For answers see p269

6. Complete the album title: *Picture* _____.

a. *Perfect*   b. *Book*   c. *Frame*

7. Simply Red twice reached No. 11 in 1987. Which of these 1987 singles did not achieve that feat?

a. 'The Right Thing'   b. 'Infidelity'

c. 'Ev'ry Time We Say Goodbye'

8. Where does Mick Hucknall call 'Home'?

a. Manchester   b. Newcastle   c. Kingston-Upon-Hull

9. In 1989, Simply Red scored their first No. 1 album. Name it.

a. *A New Flame*   b. *A New Game*   c. *A New Name*

10. How many weeks did the No. 2 album *Men And Women* stay on the chart?

a. 6   b. 60   c. 606

For answers see p269

POWER BALLADS

1. The single 'Drive' was first released in 1984, charting at No. 5, and then re-released in 1985, when it got to No. 4. Name the band.

    a. The Cars   *b.* Foreigner   *c.* REO Speedwagon

2. Foreigner scored two Top 10 hits in the UK, 'I Want To Know What Love Is' and which other ballad?

    a. 'You Give Love A Bad Name'

    b. 'Waiting For A Girl Like You'   *c.* 'Babe'

3. Who injected some 'Poison' into the singles chart?

    a. Alice Cooper   *b.* Marillion   *c.* Bon Jovi

4. What did Cher wish she could do in 1989?

    a. 'Turn The Beat Around'

    b. 'Turn Off The Light'

    c. 'Turn Back Time'

5. Who were 'Alone' in 1987?

    a. Wilson Phillips   *b.* Heart   *c.* Starship

For answers see p270

6. **Name the lead singer of the Cutting Crew, who hit the Top 5 in 1986 with '(I Just) Died In Your Arms'.**

   a. Richard Page   *b.* Bobby Kimball   *c.* Nick Van Eede

7. **T'Pau were named after a character from which science fiction series?**

   a. Star Trek   *b.* Doctor Who   *c.* Thunderbirds

8. **Identify the title of the 1989 hit by Swedish tunesmiths Roxette.**

   a. 'Listen To Your Heart'

   b. 'Listen To Your Mind'

   c. 'Listen To Your Body'

9. **Where does 'You're The Voice' hit-maker John Farnham hail from?**

   a. Canada   *b.* UK   *c.* Australia

10. **Toto sung about which continent in 1983?**

   a. Europe   *b.* Asia   *c.* Africa

For answers see p270

◆ SYNTH/ELECTRO

1. **What do the initials OMD stand for?**

   a. Orchestral Manoeuvres In The Dark

   b. Original Music Devotion

   c. Over My Deadbody

2. **Which Scottish singer was a member of both Visage and Ultravox?**

   a. Ricky Ross   b. Billy Connolly   c. Midge Ure

3. **Glenn Gregory was a member of which 'heavenly' group?**

   a. Feels Like Heaven   b. Heaven 17

   c. Heaven Is A Place On Earth

4. **Who was the female vocalist with Yazoo?**

   a. Clare Grogan   b. Alison Moyet   c. Toyah Willcox

5. **'Poison Arrow' and 'The Look Of Love' were hits for whom?**

   a. Gary Numan   b. The Human League   c. ABC

For answers see p270

6.   **What nationality were Kraftwerk?**

      a. German   *b.* French   *c.* Belgian

7.   **Whose name means 'fashion dispatch' in French?**

      a. Visage   *b.* Depeche Mode   *c.* Ultravox

8.   ***Please, Disco*** **and** ***Actually*****: all '80s albums for which duo?**

      a. Soft Cell   *b.* Yazoo   *c.* Pet Shop Boys

9.   **Who had Top 10 hits in the '80s with four different groups?**

      a. Philip Oakey   *b.* Vince Clarke   *c.* Marc Almond

10.   **Name The Human League's follow-up album to** ***Dare*****?**

      a. Hysteria   *b.* Crash   *c.* Travelogue

For answers see p270

COVER VERSIONS

1. **George Benson earlier recorded a No. 1 hit from 1988. Name It.**

   a. 'Nothing's Gonna Change My Love For You'

   b. 'One Moment In Time'   *c.* 'The Only Way Is Up'

2. **Some of the Isley Brothers wrote and originally recorded which 1986 No. 1?**

   a. 'Reet Petite (The Sweetest Girl In Town)'

   b. 'Spirit In The Sky'   *c.* 'Caravan Of Love'

3. **Who had the first hit with Jason Donovan's 'Sealed With A Kiss'?**

   a. Bobby Vee   *b.* Bobby Darin   *c.* Brian Hyland

4. **The first singer to chart with 'La Bamba' perished on the 'day the music died'. Name him.**

   a. The Big Bopper   *b.* Ritchie Valens   *c.* Buddy Holly

5. **Who had the original hit with the charity No. 1 'Ferry 'Cross The Mersey'?**

   a. The Beatles   *b.* Gerry & The Pacemakers

   c. The Merseybeats

For answers see p270

6. **Which soul star first recorded Paul Young's 'Wherever I Lay My Hat (That's My Home)'?**

   a. Sam Cooke   *b.* Otis Redding   *c.* Marvin Gaye

7. **Name the song that Elvis Presley charted with before the Pet Shop Boys.**

   a. 'It's A Sin'   *b.* 'Always On My Mind'   *c.* 'Heart'

8. **Which Motown act hit the chart in the 1960s with 'You Can't Hurry Love', later covered by Phil Collins?**

   a. Martha & The Vandellas

   b. Mary Wells

   c. The Supremes

9. **In the 1960s, Patti Labelle originally recorded which '80s chart-topping song as a B-side?**

   a. 'Ride On Time'

   b. 'A Groovy Kind Of Love'

   c. 'Move Closer'

10. **Shakin' Stevens's 'This Ole House' was a hit for which female in the '50s?**

    a. Rosemary Clooney   *b.* Alma Cogan   *c.* Lita Roza

For answers see p270

1981

1.   **What was the name of Ultravox's first Top 20 single?**

   a. 'All Stood Still'   *b.* 'The Thin Wall'   *c.* 'Vienna'

2.   **Who had their last Top 20 hit with 'You Better You Bet'?**

   a. Motörhead   *b.* Thin Lizzy   *c.* The Who

3.   **Which ensemble were 'Hooked On Classics' in this year?**

   a. Royal Philharmonic Orchestra   *b.* Sky   *c.* Dr Hook

4.   **What was hit-maker Toyah's surname before she married?**

   a. Fripp   *b.* Turner   *c.* Willcox

5.   **Complete this Cliff Richard title: '_____ Home'.**

   a. I'm   *b.* She's   *c.* Daddy's

For answers see p271

6. **David Grant, now known as the voice coach on TV talent shows, was in which popular 1981 band?**

   a. Beggar & Co.   *b.* Linx   *c.* Light Of The World

7. **Who sang 'When She Was My Girl' and 'Don't Walk Away' in 1981?**

   a. The Temptations   *b.* Alexander O'Neal   *c.* The Four Tops

8. **Who took us 'Back To The Sixties' with their first hit?**

   a. Tight Fit   *b.* Gidea Park   *c.* Modern Romance

9. **A cousin of Paul McCartney had a big hit in 1981. Name the act.**

   a. Kate Robbins & Beyond

   b. Fred Wedlock   *c.* Mary McCartney

10. **Which of the following is a true statement about Red Sovine, who made his chart debut with the CB radio song 'Teddy Bear'?**

   a. He actually was a truck driver

   b. It was a true story about his nephew

   c. He had died a year earlier

For answers see p271

◆ COMPLETE THE TITLE
ALBUMS

1. *The Number Of The _____* (Iron Maiden)

   a. Beast   b. Cab   c. Door

2. *The _____ Of Love* (ABC)

   a. Book   b. Lexicon   c. Tunnel

3. *Let's _____* (David Bowie)

   a. Dance   b. Boogie   c. Jive

4. *Into The _____* (Thompson Twins)

   a. Gutter   b. Groove   c. Gap

5. *Welcome To The _____* (Frankie Goes To Hollywood)

   a. Pleasure Dome   b. Jungle   c. Hospital

For answers see p271

6. **No _____ Required** (Phil Collins)

   a. Ticket   b. Jacket   c. Monkey

7. **Our Favourite _____** (Style Council)

   a. Shop   b. Tie   c. Album

8. **Ten Good _____** (Jason Donovan)

   a. Reasons   b. Excuses   c. Answers

9. **_____ And Hum** (U2)

   a. Sing   b. Ho   c. Rattle

10. **Born In The _____** (Bruce Springsteen)

   a. USA   b. 80s   c. Ambulance

For answers see p271

1980 ALBUMS

1. **Who became the first British female artist to have a No. 1 album?**

   a. Kate Bush   *b.* Hazel O'Connor   *c.* Marti Webb

2. **Which rock act charted with *Ace Of Spades*?**

   a. Deep Purple   *b.* Ozzy Osbourne   *c.* Motörhead

3. **Who had a smash with *Glass Houses*?**

   a. Elvis Costello   *b.* Eric Clapton   *c.* Billy Joel

4. **Name UB40's first hit album.**

   a. Signing On   *b.* Signing Off   *c.* Signing On Day

5. **Who was the star of the movie soundtrack *The Jazz Singer*?**

   a. Louis Armstrong   *b.* Neil Diamond   *c.* Barbra Streisand

For answers see p271

6. **Who were *Kings Of The Wild Frontier*?**

    a. Duran Duran   *b.* Adam & The Ants

    c. Dexy's Midnight Runners

7. **Ex-Buggles members Trevor Horn and Geoff Downes joined which top-selling album act?**

    a. Iron Maiden   *b.* 10CC   *c.* Yes

8. **Complete this David Bowie album title: *Scary Monsters (And _____).***

    a. Spiders From Mars   *b.* Super Creeps   *c.* Diamond Dogs

9. **Which Canadian act had a Top 10 album called *Permanent Waves*?**

    a. Bryan Adams   *b.* Celine Dion   *c.* Rush

10. ***Duke* was the first No. 1 album by which regular chart act?**

    a. David Bowie   *b.* Genesis   *c.* Duke Ellington

For answers see p271

MICHAEL JACKSON

1. **'Happy (Love Theme From ___)'**

   a. A Star Is Born   b. Mahogany   c. Lady Sings The Blues

2. **'___ Girl'**

   a. Libyan   b. Liberian   c. Namibian

3. **'Dirty ___'**

   a. Diana   b. Joanna   c. Hannah

4. **'She's Out Of My ___**

   a. Life   b. Reach   c. League

5. **'The Girl Is ___'**

   a. Mine   b. Wild   c. Fine

For answers see p272

6. **'Smooth _____'**

         a. Talker   *b.* Dresser   *c.* Criminal

7. **'P.Y.T. (_____)'**

         a. People You're Terrific   *b.* Places You've Travelled

         c. Pretty Young Thing

8. **'Girl You're So _____'**

         a. Together   *b.* Beautiful   *c.* Strange

9. **'_____ In The Mirror'**

         a. Face   *b.* Man   *c.* Stranger

10. **_____ (1981 single and album)**

         a. 'One Day In Your Life'   *b.* 'Bad'   *c.* 'Billie Jean'

For answers see p272

1982

1. **Who had hits with 'Go Wild In The Country' and 'I Want Candy'?**

   a. Culture Club   *b.* Duran Duran   *c.* Bow Wow Wow

2. **Kim Wilde had 'A View From A _____'?**

   a. Bridge   *b.* Window   *c.* Cliff

3. **Blancmange had the first of four Top 20 hits with which song?**

   a. 'Living On The Ceiling'   *b.* 'Waves'   *c.* 'Don't Tell Me'

4. **Where did Gary Numan 'Take Mystery To'?**

   a. Heaven   *b.* Bed   *c.* Hell

5. **Who had no regrets pursuing a solo career in 1982?**

   a. Marc Almond   *b.* Gary Numan   *c.* Midge Ure

For answers see p272

6. **What was the name of The Stranglers' biggest hit single?**

   a. 'Strange Little Girl'

   b. 'Golden Brown'

   c. 'European Female'

7. **Name the ex-roadie who hit the chart with 'Arthur's Theme'?**

   a. Meat Loaf b. Christopher Cross c. Eddy Grant

8. **What was the name of Fat Larry's Band's only Top 20 entry?**

   a. 'Zoom' b. 'Boom' c. 'Doom'

9. **'Oh Diane' was a Top 10 hit for whom this year?**

   a. Associates b. A Flock Of Seagulls c. Fleetwood Mac

10. **'I'm A Wonderful Thing (Baby)' introduced us to which act?**

   a. Kid Creole & The Coconuts

   b. Kool & The Gang

   c. Rocker's Revenge

For answers see p272

FILL IN THE GAPS
PLACES

1. 'The _____' (The Human League)

2. 'Dolce Vita' (Ryan _____)

3. 'One Night In _____' (Murray Head)

4. 'Big In _____' (Alphaville)

5. 'Christian' (_____ Crisis)

6. 'This Is Not _____' (David Bowie & The Pat Metheny Group)

7. 'Relax' (Frankie Goes To _____)

8. 'A New _____' (Kirsty MacColl)

9. 'Tour De _____' (Kraftwerk)

10. 'Come To _____' (The Style Council)

Bangkok   France   Hollywood   Paris

England   China   America   Lebanon

Milton Keynes   Japan

For answers see p272

1983

1. **Name the first single by the Eurythmics to reach the Top 20.**

   a. 'Love Is A Stranger'   b. 'Sweet Dreams'

   c. 'Who's That Girl?'

2. **What kind of summer did Bananarama have?**

   a. Lovely   b. Sad   c. Cruel

3. **Siouxsie & The Banshees hit the chart with which Beatles song?**

   a. 'Here, There & Everywhere'   b. 'Dear Prudence'

   c. 'With A Little Help From My Friends'

4. **Which act had 15 different singles in the Top 100 simultaneously?**

   a. Elvis Presley   b. The Beatles   c. The Jam

5. **What was Bob Marley's biggest hit of the year?**

   a. 'Buffalo Soldier'   b. 'One Love/People Get Ready'

   c. 'No Woman No Cry'

6. **What was the title of Keith Harris & Orville's biggest hit?**

   a. 'Orville's Tune'   b. 'Orville's Song'   c. 'Orville's Melody'

7. **What did Motown Records celebrate this year?**

   a. Their 10th UK No. 1   b. Their 25th anniversary

   c. The 50th birthday of owner Berry Gordy

For answers see p273

8. Complete the title of this Men Without Hats hit: 'The _____ Dance'.

    a. Happy   *b.* Silly   *c.* Safety

9. David Essex had his last Top 20 hit with which song?

    a. 'A Winter's Tale'   *b.* 'Tahiti'   *c.* 'Me And My Girl'

10. Name the band Vince Clarke formed after leaving Yazoo.

    a. The Assembly   *b.* Depeche Mode   *c.* Wah!

For answers see p273

COVER VERSIONS

1. **T-Rex star Marc Bolan's girlfriend, Gloria Jones, recorded the original version of which '80s chart-topping song?**

   a. 'Being With You'   b. 'Tainted Love'

   c. 'Together We Are Beautiful'

2. **Who had the biggest UK hit in the '50s with Shakin' Stevens's No. 1 'Green Door'?**

   a. Tommy Steele   b. Marty Wilde   c. Frankie Vaughan

3. **Alison Moyet had a big hit with a song previously charted by Elvis Presley. What was it?**

   a. 'That Ole Devil Called Love'

   b. 'Love Letters'

   c. 'All Cried Out'

4. **The Chi-Lites' 'Too Good To Be Forgotten' was taken into the Top 5 in 1986 by which group?**

   a. Bananarama   b. The Bangles   c. Amazulu

5. **Which '60s US band had the original recording of Tiffany's hit 'I Think We're Alone Now'?**

   a. Gary Puckett & The Union Gap

   b. Tommy James & The Shondells

   c. Gary Lewis & The Playboys

6. **The Tokens had a US No. 1 with which '80s chart-topping song?**

   a. 'Frankie'   b. 'Uptown Girl'   c. 'The Lion Sleeps Tonight'

For answers see p273

7. **Amii Stewart's disco hit 'Knock On Wood' was first recorded by which Stax artist?**

   a. Otis Redding   *b.* Eddie Floyd   *c.* Sam & Dave

8. **In 1982, Bad Manners revived 'My Boy Lollipop'. Who had a hit with it in the '60s?**

   a. Millie   *b.* Lulu   *c.* Twinkle

9. **Which of these Bananarama hits is not a cover version?**

   a. 'Venus'   *b.* 'Cruel Summer'

   c. 'Na Na Hey Hey Kiss Him Goodbye'

10. **The Beat's 'Tears Of A Clown' was originally a hit for which group?**

    a. The Four Tops

    b. Smokey Robinson & The Miracles

    c. The Temptations

For answers see p273

DANCE

1. **Midge Ure replaced John Foxx as frontman of which group?**

   a. Classix Nouveaux   *b.* Visage   *c.* Ultravox

2. **What was the first Human League single to reach the Top 10 in the UK?**

   a. 'Mirror Man'

   b. 'Love Action (I Believe In Love)'

   c. 'The Lebanon'

3. **How many members of Duran Duran had the surname Taylor?**

   a. Three   *b.* Four   *c.* Two

4. **Vince Clarke, a member of Yazoo, then Erasure, first tasted chart success with which Basildon foursome?**

   a. Culture Club   *b.* Depeche Mode

   c. Blue Rondo A La Turk

5. **From which controversial 1971 film did Heaven 17 get their name?**

   a. The Devils   *b.* Straw Dogs   *c.* A Clockwork Orange

6. **'Tainted Love' was a No. 1 hit all around the world for which duo?**

   a. Talk Talk   *b.* Soft Cell   *c.* Blancmange

7. **What was the name of ABC's lead singer?**

   a. Martin Fry   *b.* Tom Bailey   *c.* Simon Le Bon

For answers see p273

8. In which year did Culture Club make their chart debut in Britain?

a. 1980   b. 1982   c. 1984

9. Which chart-topping group released singles called 'To Cut A Long Story Short', 'True' and 'Gold'?

a. The Mobiles   b. Ca Va Ca Va   c. Spandau Ballet

10. Which British group's LP releases included *Tin Drum, Oil On Canvas* and *Quiet Life*?

a. Haysi Fantayzee   b. Japan   c. Kissing The Pink

For answers see p273

1984

1. **Complete this sentence: In the US, Michael Jackson's 'Farewell My Summer Love'** _____ .

   a. Was a No. 1   *b.* Sold over a million

   c. Did not make the Top 20

2. ***Purple Rain, Beat Street*** and ***Breakdance*** were what?

   a. Titles of No. 1 albums   *b.* Titles of 1983 films

   c. Tracks by Prince

3. **Who felt like Buddy Holly this year?**

   a. David Essex   *b.* Shakin' Stevens   *c.* Alvin Stardust

4. **What happened to Michael Jackson when he was filming an ad for Pepsi?**

   a. He lost his famous glove

   b. He twisted his ankle moonwalking

   c. His hair caught fire

5. **What was the year's biggest-selling single that did not reach No. 1?**

   a. 'Radio Ga Ga' – Queen

   b. 'Last Christmas' – Wham!

   c. 'The Wild Boys' – Duran Duran

For answers see p274

6. **Rockers Jimmy Page and Paul Rodgers formed a group called what?**

   a. The Honeydrippers

   b. The Firm

   c. The Page Rodgers Band

7. **In the title of the Pointer Sisters' hit, which words are in brackets after 'Jump'?**

   a. (To The Beat)   b. (For My Love)   c. (For Joy)

8. **Why was Renate Blauel in the news?**

   a. She took a shot at Michael Jackson

   b. She married Elton John

   c. She invented the CD

9. **Complete this Echo & The Bunnymen title: 'The Killing _____'.**

   a. Fields   b. Moon   c. Spree

10. **What was the most popular music-related T-shirt theme?**

   a. Boy George Loves. . .

   b. Duran Duran Dig. . .

   c. Frankie Says. . .

For answers see p274

ONE-HIT WONDERS
NAME THE YEAR OF THEIR ONLY TOP 20 HIT

1. Keith Harris & Orville, Men Without Hats, Flash And The Pan, The Maisonettes

2. The Crowd, DeBarge, Harold Faltermeyer, Colonel Abrams

3. Laurie Anderson, Fred Wedlock, Coast To Coast, Champaign

4. Robin Beck, Harry Enfield, Sabrina, Angry Anderson

5. Nina, Neil, Joe Fagin, John Waite

6. Black Slate, The Vapors, Stephanie Mills, M*A*S*H

7. Liza Minnelli, Damian, Jeff Wayne, Midnight Oil

8. M/A/R/R/S, Spagna, Robbie Nevil, Iggy Pop

9. Charlene, Bardo, David Christie, Christopher Cross

10. Anita Dobson, Grange Hill Cast, Doctor & The Medics, Double

1980   1981   1982   1983

1984   1985   1986   1987

1988   1989

For answers see p274

 **1981 ALBUMS**

1. **Who was *Wired For Sound*?**

    a. Echo & The Bunnymen

    b. Electric Light Orchestra

    c. Cliff Richard

2. ***The Friends Of Mr Cairo* was a hit album for which act?**

    a. Joy Division   *b.* Jon & Vangelis   *c.* OMD

3. ***Almost Blue* and *Trust* were hits this year for which act?**

    a. The Moody Blues   *b.* Rod Stewart   *c.* Elvis Costello

4. **Which act spent 15 weeks at No. 1 in the US with *Hi-Infidelity*?**

    a. Journey   *b.* Styx   *c.* REO Speedwagon

5. **Who took you at *Face Value*?**

    a. Queen   *b.* Phil Collins   *c.* Simon & Garfunkel

For answers see p274

6. **Complete this sentence: Starsound were the first group from _____ to top the albums chart.**

   a. Norway   b. The Netherlands   c. Italy

7. **Which British female had her most successful album with** *Pearls*?

   a. Kate Bush   b. Elkie Brooks   c. Joan Armatrading

8. **Bruce Dickinson from Samson joined which top-selling album act?**

   a. Def Leppard   b. Iron Maiden   c. AC/DC

9. **Complete this Spandau Ballet album title:** *Journey To _____.*

   a. Glory   b. The Stars   c. The Centre Of The Earth

10. ***Shot Of Love* was a hit album in 1981 for which chart regular?**

    a. The Rolling Stones   b. Status Quo   c. Bob Dylan

For answers see p274

 **1985**

1. **Which act appeared in the Live Aid shows in both London and Philadelphia?**

   a. Queen   *b.* Elton John   *c.* Phil Collins

2. **Name the first hit by a-ha.**

   a. 'Take On Me'

   b. 'The Sun Always Shines On TV'

   c. 'Train Of Thought'

3. **Who bought the music publishing rights to The Beatles' songs?**

   a. Paul McCartney   *b.* George Martin   *c.* Michael Jackson

4. **Who picked up the BRIT award for Best British Male Singer?**

   a. George Michael   *b.* Paul Young   *c.* Phil Collins

5. **Which one-hit wonder had a Top 5 single with 'Obsession'?**

   a. The Far Corporation   *b.* Opus   *c.* Animotion

For answers see p275

6. **George Harrison, Eric Clapton and Ringo Starr backed which '50s rocker on TV?**

   a. Jerry Lee Lewis   b. Little Richard   c. Carl Perkins

7. **The singer they called 'The Boss' had a very successful tour in this year. Name him.**

   a. Diana Ross   b. Frank Sinatra   c. Bruce Springsteen

8. **What was the name of Jimmy Nail's first hit?**

   a. 'Love Don't Live Here Anymore'

   b. 'Crocodile Shoes'

   c. 'Ain't No Doubt'

9. **Who were the first Western group to play live in China?**

   a. Frankie Goes To Hollywood   b. Japan   c. Wham!

10. **Who gave us a 'History' lesson?**

    a. Tina Turner   b. Bucks Fizz   c. Mai Tai

For answers see p275

FILL IN THE GAPS
OCCUPATIONS

1. 'The Living Years' (Mike & The _____)

2. Buffalo _____' (Bob Marly & The Wailers)

3. 'Sweet Love' (Anita _____)

4. '_____' (Smiley Culture)

5. '_____'s Blues' (The Waterboys)

6. 'Lies' (Jonathan _____)

7. 'Drop The _____' (Joan Armatrading)

8. 'We Are _____' (Thompson Twins)

9. 'Burn' (_____ & The Medics)

10. '_____ Of Orleans' (O.M.D.)

Pilot   Baker   Butler   Mechanics

Soldier   Maid   Doctor   Detective

Police Officer   Fisherman

For answers see p275

COMPLETE THE TITLE SINGLES

1. 'And The _____ Goes On' (The Whispers)

     a. Dance   *b.* Music   *c.* Beat

2. 'What's Another _____' (Johnny Logan)

     a. Boy   *b.* Year   *c.* Dance

3. 'Stars On _____' (Starsound)

     a. Drugs   *b.* Broadway   *c.* 45

4. 'How 'Bout _____' (Champaign)

     a. Love   *b.* Us   *c.* It

5. 'My _____ Never Lies' (Bucks Fizz)

     a. Girl   *b.* Heart   *c.* Camera

6. 'I've Never Been To _____' (Charlene)

     a. Spain   *b.* LA   *c.* Me

7. 'Moonlight _____' (Mike Oldfield)

     a. Shadow   *b.* Night   *c.* Love

8. 'New _____' (Howard Jones)

     a. Hat   *b.* Guitar   *c.* Song

9. 'Two _____' (Frankie Goes To Hollywood)

     a. Lovers   *b.* Timer   *c.* Tribes

10. 'When _____ Cry' (Prince)

     a. Girls   *b.* Boys   *c.* Doves

For answers see p275

GIRL POWER
MATCH THE LADIES AND THEIR TOP 10 HITS

1. Belinda Carlisle

2. Bonnie Tyler

3. Amii Stewart

4. Cher

5. Aneka

6. Carly Simon

7. Alison Moyet

8. Cyndi Lauper

9. Charlene

10. Barbra Streisand

'Japanese Boy'   'Coming Around Again'   'All Cried Out'

'I Drove All Night'   'I Found Someone'   'Woman In Love'

'Knock On Wood'/'Light My Fire'   'Total Eclipse Of The Heart'

'I've Never Been To Me'   'Circle In The Sand'

For answers see p276

ORIGINATES FROM

MATCH THE TOP 10 ACT AND THE COUNTRY THEY CAME FROM

1. a-ha

2. Ennio Morricone

3. Berlin

4. Alphaville

5. Boris Gardiner

6. Edelweiss

7. David Christie

8. Angry Anderson

9. Double

10. Baltimora

Italy   Austria   Switzerland   France

USA   Jamaica   Ireland   Australia

Germany   Norway

For answers see p276

GUESS THE SONG

1. Dexy's Midnight Runners performed which song on *Top Of The Pops* accompanied by a picture of darts player Jocky Wilson?

    a. 'Come On Eileen'   *b.* 'Geno'

    c. 'Jackie Wilson Said (I'm In Heaven When You Smile)'

2. The Smiths released their first (non-charting) single in May 1983. What was it called?

    a. 'Hand In Pocket'   *b.* 'Hand In The Till'   *c.* 'Hand In Glove'

3. The video for which Kim Wilde single was banned for being 'too saucy'?

    a. 'Say You Really Want Me'

    b. 'Four Letter Word'

    c. 'Chequered Love'

4. In 1986, George Michael wrote, arranged, produced, sang and played all the instruments on which No. 1 track?

    a. 'Careless Whisper'   *b.* 'A Different Corner'   *c.* 'Faith'

5. The unusual pairing of Eartha Kitt and Bronski Beat teamed up on which moderately successful 1989 single?

    a. 'You Make Me Feel (Mighty Real)'

    b. 'Cha Cha Heels'

    c. 'Under The Bridges Of Paris'

For answers see p277

6. **Which Salt-n-Pepa song was released as a double A-side with first 'I Am Down' and then 'Tramp' in 1988?**

a. 'Expression'   b. 'Push It'

c. 'Shake Your Thang (It's Your Thing)'

7. **Which quizzical song by Nik Kershaw features an aged gentleman from Aran, who goes in circles around a hole in the ground?**

a. 'Love Of The Common People'

b. 'The Riddle'

c. 'New Song'

8. **What did Erasure want in 1988?**

a. 'An Alien For Christmas'

b. 'Freedom'

c. 'A Little Respect'

9. **Complete the title of this Firm single: '_____ (E's Alright)'.**

a. David Jason   b. Ronnie Barker   c. Arthur Daley

10. **Which Squeeze hit was released in the '80s?**

a. 'Cool For Cats'

b. 'Labelled With Love'

c. 'Up The Junction'

For answers see p277

1986

1. Complete the title of this Grange Hill Cast hit: 'Just Say _____'.

   a. Yes   b. OK   c. No

2. Who sang 'The Captain Of Her Heart'?

   a. Double   b. Captain & Tennille   c. Captain Sensible

3. The musical *Time* opened in London in 1986. Who was the star?

   a. David Cassidy   b. Cliff Richard   c. David Essex

4. Frank Sinatra had his last solo Top 10 hit this year. Name it.

   a. 'My Way'   b. 'New York, New York'

   c. 'Love's Been Good To Me'

5. Name Chris De Burgh's first Top 20 entry.

   a. 'The Lady In Red'

   b. 'Don't Pay The Ferryman'

   c. 'Missing You'

For answers see p277

6. **Who sang with Cherrelle on 'Saturday Love' in January 1986?**

   a. Luther Vandross   *b.* Alexander O'Neal   *c.* Al Jarreau

7. **Who wrote and recorded the new *Top Of The Pops* theme?**

   a. Thin Lizzy   *b.* Paul Hardcastle   *c.* Peter Gabriel

8. **Which act had the hit record associated with the charity Race Against Time in 1986?**

   a. Status Quo   *b.* Eurythmics   *c.* Tears For Fears

9. **Whitney Houston's 'Greatest Love Of All' was first recorded by which R&B star?**

   a. George Benson   *b.* Al Jarreau   *c.* Luther Vandross

10. **What percentage of New Zealand's population saw Dire Straits' 1986 tour?**

    a. 8%   *b.* 28%   *c.* 58%

For answers see p277

COVER VERSIONS

1. **Harold Melvin & The Bluenotes originally recorded which 1986 No. 1?**

    a. 'When The Going Gets Tough'

    b. 'Don't Leave Me This Way'

    c. 'I Want To Wake Up With You'

2. **The Crowd's No. 1 'You'll Never Walk Alone' orginally came from what musical?**

    a. The Sound Of Music   *b.* Carousel   *c.* The King & I

3. **Who produced the original Lesley Gore version of Dave Stewart & Barbara Gaskin's No. 1 'It's My Party'?**

    a. Phil Spector   *b.* Quincy Jones   *c.* George Martin

4. **Which Motown act had the first hit with the David Bowie & Mick Jagger No. 1 'Dancing In The Street'?**

    a. The Marvelettes   *b.* The Supremes

    c. Martha & The Vandellas

5. **Which group took the Four Seasons original 'Working My Way Back To You' to the top?**

    a. The Detroit Spinners

    b. The Detroit Emeralds

    c. Odyssey

For answers see p277

6. **Doctor & The Medics' 'Spirit In The Sky' was originally a No. 1 hit for?**

   a. Edwin Hawkins Singers   *b.* Dave Edmunds

   c. Norman Greenbaum

7. **Don McLean's 'Crying ' was first a hit by Roy Orbison in what year?**

   a. 1965   *b.* 1961   *c.* 1964

8. **What was the name of the act that took The Beatles' 'Let It Be' to the top in 1987?**

   a. Ferry Good   *b.* Ferry Trip   *c.* Ferry Aid

9. **Yazoo's 1982 hit 'Only You' was a big hit a year later by what act?**

   a. The Flying Lizards

   b. Flying Burrito Brothers

   c. The Flying Pickets

10. **Diana Ross's 1981 Top 5 hit 'Why Do Fools Fall In Love' was a No. 1 for which act in 1956?**

    a. The Teenagers featuring Frankie Lymon

    b. Paul Anka   *c.* Del Shannon

For answers see p277

◎ MATCH THE TOP 10 GROUP AND THEIR SINGER

1. XTC

2. Yazoo

3. Pet Shop Boys

4. Nena

5. The Pretenders

6. Sade

7. OMD

8. Simple Minds

9. Opus

10. Prefab Sprout

Helen Folasade Adu   Herwig Rüdisser

Andy McCluskey   Chrissie Hynde   Jim Kerr

Paddy McAloon   Gabriele Kerner   Andy Partridge

Alison Moyet   Neil Tennant

For answers see p278

R&B

1. **Who had the 'Midas Touch' in 1986?**

   a. Atlantic Starr   *b.* Midnight Star   *c.* Starsound

2. **Chaka Khan sang with which group on the Top 10 hit 'Ain't Nobody'?**

   a. Aurra   *b.* The Chaka-Lettes   *c.* Rufus

3. **Complete the title of this 1988 Mica Paris hit: 'My One _____'.**

   a. And Only   *b.* Desire   *c.* Temptation

4. **In 1989 who had a Top 10 hit with 'I Need Your Lovin'?**

   a. Chanelle   *b.* Alyson Williams   *c.* Donna Allen

5. **Who was 'On My Own' with Michael McDonald in 1986?**

   a. Gladys Knight   *b.* Dionne Warwick   *c.* Patti Labelle

6. **Who was 'Going Back To My Roots' in 1981?**

   a. Odyssey   *b.* The Whispers   *c.* Heatwave

7. **What instrument does 'The Groove' hit-maker Rodney Franklin play?**

   a. Keyboards   *b.* Drums   *c.* Bass

8. **Who drove up the singles chart with their 'Pink Cadillac' in 1988?**

   a. Stephanie Mills   *b.* Natalie Cole   *c.* Womack & Womack

For answers see p278

9. Who had a 'king' size hit with 'Say I'm Your Number One' in 1985?

   a. Prince   *b.* Princess   *c.* Queen

10. Berry Gordy's son, Kennedy, charted with 'Somebody's Watching You' under what name?

   a. Berry's Boy   *b.* The Son Of Gordy   *c.* Rockwell

For answers see p278

1987

1. What year did Nina Simone record her 1986 hit 'My Baby Just Cares For Me'?

   a. 1967 *b.* 1977 *c.* 1957

2. Complete the name of this hit act: Mental As _____.

   a. Can Be *b.* Anything *c.* A Pop Quiz Contestant

3. Which act was voted Best British Group at the BRIT awards?

   a. Five Star *b.* Dire Straits *c.* Eurythmics

4. Australian superstar John Farnham's only UK hit was 'You're The _____'.

   a. One *b.* Girl *c.* Voice

5. Rapper Ad Rock received some negative UK press coverage during his group's tour. Name the group.

   a. Run-DMC *b.* Public Enemy *c.* Beastie Boys

6. Who took us to 'The Circus' this year?

   a. Pet Shop Boys *b.* Erasure *c.* The Jesus & Mary Chain

7. Just before he died, pop artist Andy Warhol directed a video for which act?

   a. a-ha *b.* Madonna *c.* Curiosity Killed The Cat

8. Complete this Cliff Richard Top 10 title: 'My _____ One'.

   a. Little *b.* Pretty *c.* Only

For answers see p278

9. Who sent 'Love Letters' this year?

    a. Randy Crawford   *b.* Alison Moyet   *c.* Whitney Houston

10. Which UK act walked away with a Grammy for Top Single?

    a. Steve Winwood   *b.* Phil Collins   *c.* Tears For Fears

For answers see p278

1982 ALBUMS

1. **John Wetton and Steve Howe were members of which top-selling album act?**

   a. Yes   *b.* King Crimson   *c.* Asia

2. **Complete the name of the act who released the album *Love And Dancing*: The _____ Unlimited Orchestra.**

   a. Love   *b.* Electric   *c.* League

3. ***Business As Usual* was the top album in the US this year. Who was it by?**

   a. Asia   *b.* John Cougar   *c.* Men At Work

4. ***In The Name Of Love* was an album from which act?**

   a. The Proclaimers   *b.* Thompson Twins   *c.* Bros

5. **Complete the sentence: In their homeland, The Kids From Fame _____.**

   a. Earned three gold albums

   b. Never charted in the Top 40

   c. Had two No. 1 albums

6. **Which singer won a Grammy for their 1982 *Love Songs* album?**

   a. Barry Manilow   *b.* Barbra Streisand   *c.* Dolly Parton

7. **Who was *Upstairs At Eric's*?**

   a. Yazoo   *b.* Visage   *c.* Simple Minds

For answers see p279

8. *Dare* was the album by the act voted Best Newcomer at the BRIT Awards. Name the act.

   a. Depeche Mode   *b.* The Human League   *c.* Soft Cell

9. Bruce Springsteen's hit album this year was called what?

   a. Ohio   *b.* Nebraska   *c.* Delaware

10. Complete the title of this Culture Club album: _____ *To Be Clever*.

    a. Studying   *b.* Learning   *c.* Kissing

For answers see p279

GIRL POWER
SINGLES

1. **In which northern town was Lisa Stansfield born in 1966?**

   a. Rochdale   *b.* Carlisle   *c.* Grimsby

2. **'Together We Are Beautiful' was recorded by which American singer?**

   a. Katrina Leskanich   *b.* Fern Kinney   *c.* Debbie Harry

3. **Which singer/actress married Big Audio Dynamite's Dan Donovan in 1988?**

   a. Anita Dobson   *b.* Patsy Kensit   *c.* Jennifer Saunders

4. **How many Top 10 singles did Toyah Willcox have in 1981?**

   a. None   *b.* Three   *c.* Eight

5. **On which page of the *Sun* newspaper did Sam Fox appear under the headline 'Sam, 16, Quits A-Levels for Ooh-Levels' in February 1983?**

   a. Front page   *b.* Page 3   *c.* Page 17

6. **What is Kim Wilde's only UK chart-topping single?**

   a. 'Kids In America'

   b. 'You Keep Me Hangin' On'

   c. She's never had a UK No. 1

7. **Toni Basil's 'Mickey' is a cover version of a song recorded (from a male perspective) by Racey in 1979. Name it.**

   a. 'Kitty'   *b.* 'Vicky'   *c.* 'Nicky'

For answers see p279

8. **Where was former Go-Go Jane Wiedlin driving in 1988?**

    a. 'In The Country'

    b. 'Away From Home'

    c. (In the) 'Rush Hour'

9. **What type of sea creature did the B-52s sing about?**

    a. Rock lobster   b. Rockin' crab   c. Rocktopus

10. **Originally from the 1928 film *Whoopee*, which Nina Simone song made the Top 5 in 1987 following its use in a perfume advert?**

    a. 'My Baby Just Cares For Me'

    b. 'Feeling Good'   c. 'Blue For You'

For answers see p279

GENIUS ROUND

1. John Lennon & The Muscle Shoals Horns, Millie Jackson, Dionne Warwick & Friends, Stevie Wonder, Gladys Knight, Cliff Richard, Jennifer Rush, _____. Who completes this list?

    a. Aretha Franklin   *b.* Marvin Gaye   *c.* Smokey Robinson

2. Name the guitarist and bass player who link '80s acts The Beat, Fine Young Cannibals and Two Men, A Drum Machine And A Trumpet.

    a. Dave Wakeling and Mike Barson

    b. Andy Cox and David Steele

    c. Roland Gift and John Bradbury

3. What two weather conditions are described as 'prisoners too' in the heartbreaking '80s ballad 'On The Inside' by Lynne Hamilton

    a. Sun and rain   *b.* Wind and snow   *c.* Sleet and hail

4. 'Loving Arms', 'The Sound Of Your Cry', 'Baby I Don't Care', 'The Last Farewell'. Name the singer.

    a. Transvision Vamp   *b.* Billie Ray Martin   *c.* Elvis Presley

5. Rock legends Joe Strummer and Gene Simmons were born in which countries respectively?

    a. Turkey and Israel

    b. Mexico and Argentina

    c. Morocco and Algeria

For answers see p279

6. Members of which band were born on 17 July 1985, 23 December 1985, 12 March 1986 and 30 November 1987?

       a. Girls Aloud   *b.* McFly   *c.* Westlife

7. Which group was the first to score four Top 20 hits off an album in the '80s?

       a. ABBA   *b.* ABC   *c.* AC/DC

8. Shakin' Stevens was the most successful chart act of the '80s. How many singles did the hip-swiveller rack up?

       a. 30   *b.* 40   *c.* 50

9. How many words make up the full name of the Birmingham-based all-girl pop punk quartet fronted by Vickie Perks?

       a. 6   *b.* 9   *c.* 12

10. In 1986, what equalled MC^2?

       a. B   *b.* C   *c.* E

For answers see p279

GIRL POWER
ALBUMS

1. **Kate Bush scored five Top 3 albums in the '80s. The first of these was her first No. 1. Name it.**

   a. Forever And Ever   *b.* The Dreaming   *c.* Never For Ever

2. **Alf from Essex is an apt description of which singer?**

   a. Lisa Stansfield   *b.* Wendy James   *c.* Alison Moyet

3. **Which televised event from 1988 kick-started Tracy Chapman's career?**

   a. Nelson Mandela 70th Birthday Tribute

   b. Live Aid   *c.* The Concert for Bangladesh

4. **What is the real surname of the woman who hit the top with *Anything For You* and *Cuts Both Ways*?**

   a. Estefano   *b.* Fajardo   *c.* Rubio

5. **Identify the Top 10 album released by Bananarama in 1983.**

   a. Deep Sea Skiving

   b. Deep Sea Diving

   c. Deep Sea Fishing

6. **Complete the title of this Sinead O'Connor album: *The Lion And The* _____.**

   a. Cobra   *b.* Python   *c.* Rattlesnake

For answers see p280

7. **Which year formed part of the title of Janet Jackson's *Rhythm Nation* album from 1989?**

       a. 1814   *b. 1889*   *c. 1989*

8. **Who had a *Heart Of Stone*?**

       a. Madonna   *b.* Sonia   *c.* Cher

9. **Which US No. 1 album scraped into the Top 20 for Heart in 1985?**

       a. My Iron Lung   *b. Kidney Stone*   *c. Heart*

10. **The Kirsty MacColl-penned 'They Don't Know' appeared on which 1983 Tracey Ullman album?**

       a. You Broke My Heart In 17 Places

       b. Kite   *c. Faster Than The Speed Of Night*

For answers see p280

NOVELTY/ONE-HIT WONDERS

1. **Keith Michell sang about which character in 1980?**

    a. 'Captain Beaky'

    b. 'Private Squawk'

    c. 'Sergeant Squirrel'

2. **In 1980, where would you always find Jona Lewie at parties?**

    a. In the kitchen   b. By the drinks cabinet   c. Back at home

3. **In 1989, Andy Stewart was asking: 'Donald, Where's Your _____'?**

    a. Manners   b. Troosers   c. Haggis

4. **Who sang 'The Time Warp' in 1989?**

    a. Meat Loaf   b. Richard O'Brien   c. Damian

5. **In the *M*A*S*H* theme, what was painless?**

    a. Suicide   b. Visiting the dentist   c. Acupuncture

6. **_Neighbours_ star Stefan Dennis charted with which song in 1989?**

    a. 'Don't It Make You Feel Good'

    b. 'Don't It Make You Feel Happy'

    c. 'Don't It Make You Feel Glad'

7. **DJs Pat & Mick hadn't stopped doing what in 1989?**

    a. Dancing   b. Singing   c. Clapping

For answers see p280

8. Which TV comedy actress was 'Starting Together' in 1986?

    a. Anita Dobson   *b.* Su Pollard   *c.* Judi Dench

9. In 1981, Fred Wedlock claimed to be the oldest what in town?

    a. Swinger   *b.* Morris dancer   *c.* Teenager

10. What was Weird Al Yankovic's 1984 Michael Jackson spoof called?

    a. 'Billie Joan'   *b.* 'Eat It'   *c.* 'Driller Thriller'

FILL IN THE GAPS

NUMBERS (1 to 10)

1. '_____ To 5' (Sheena Easton)

2. 'Our Lips Are Sealed' (Fun Boy _____)

3. 'Step Off (Part 1)' (Grandmaster Melle Mel & The Furious _____)

4. 'Say I'm Your Number _____' (Princess)

5. 'Be My Number _____' (Joe Jackson)

6. '_____ Pack' (The Police)

7. '_____ Letter Word' (Kim Wilde)

8. '_____ Seas' (Echo & The Bunnymen)

9. 'That's The Way Love Is' (_____ City)

10. 'I'm Not Scared' (_____th Wonder)

1   2   3   4

5   6   7   8

9   10

For answers see p280

COMPLETE THE TITLE SINGLES

1. 'Love And _____' (King)

    a. Hate   *b.* Pride   *c.* Chips

2. 'Axel _____' (Harold Faltermeyer)

    a. G   *b.* F   *c.* Grease

3. '_____ Addict' (Five Star)

    a. System   *b.* Love   *c.* Drug

4. '_____ Monday' (The Bangles)

    a. Monday   *b.* Blue   *c.* Manic

5. 'A Boy From _____' (Tom Jones)

    a. Ipanema   *b.* Nowhere   *c.* Wales

6. '_____ Your Body' (Steve 'Silk' Hurley)

    a. Jack   *b.* Move   *c.* Swing

7. 'Sign Your _____' (Terence Trent D'Arby)

    a. Card   *b.* Cheque   *c.* Name

8. 'I _____ Be So Lucky' (Kylie Minogue)

    a. Would   *b.* Could   *c.* Should

9. '_____ Life' (Inner City)

    a. Love   *b.* Good   *c.* Tough

10. 'Love _____' (Holly Johnson)

    a. Train   *b.* Hurts   *c.* You

For answers see p281

FILL IN THE GAPS
ANIMALS

1. 'Nellie The _____' (Toy Dolls)

2. '_____ Soldier' (Bob Marley & The Wailers)

3. 'We All Stand Together' (Paul McCartney & The _____ Chorus)

4. 'Wings Of A _____' (Madness)

5. 'Bring On The Dancing _____' (Echo & The Bunnymen)

6. 'Union Of The _____' (Duran Duran)

7. 'Caravan Of Love' (The _____)

8. 'Cry _____' (a-ha)

9. '_____' (Lloyd Cole & The Commotions)

10. 'Drag Me Down' (The Boomtown _____)

Buffalo   Dove   Elephant   Frog

Horses   Rats   Snake   Wolf

Rattlesnakes   Housemartins

For answers see p281

 **DUETS**

1. **Elaine Paige and Barbara Dickson's 'I Know Him So Well' was used in which Tim Rice/Benny Andersson/ Bjorn Ulvaeus musical?**

   a. Draughts   *b. Backgammon*   *c. Chess*

2. **The co-writer of 'I Knew You Were Waiting (For Me)' was one half of which late-'80s band featuring Rob Fisher?**

   a. Climie Fisher (Simon Climie)

   b. Curiosity Killed The Cat (Ben Volpeliere-Pierrot)

   c. Scritti Politti (Green Gartside)

3. **What were the stage names of British singer Hilary Lester and her Italian co-vocalist, who sang 'Save Your Love' in 1982?**

   a. Renée and Renato

   b. René and Yvette

   c. René and Angela

4. **Which single shares its name with what was the capital city of Kublai Khan's Yuan Dynasty?**

   a. 'Zabadak'   *b.* 'Zunga Zeng'   *c.* 'Xanadu'

5. **Jennifer Warnes, the queen of the '80s movie power ballad, duetted with whom on Dirty Dancing's '(I've Had) The Time Of My Life'?**

   a. Patrick Swayze   *b.* Bill Medley   *c.* Joe Cocker

For answers see p281

6. **Who was 'the other one' in Wham!?**

   a. Andrew Midgeley

   b. Andrew Pidgeley

   c. Andrew Ridgeley

7. **'Don't Give Up' was the advice from which duo in 1986?**

   a. Peter Gabriel and Kate Bush

   b. Peter Gabriel and Sheena Easton

   c. Peter Gabriel and Grace Jones

8. **Name the keyboard player who duetted with Barbara Gaskin on the 1981 smash 'It's My Party'.**

   a. Dave Stewart   b. Jermaine Stewart   c. Andy Stewart

9. **The Spike Milligan quote 'black notes, white notes, and you need to play the two to make harmony folks!' provided the inspiration for the title of which song?**

   a. 'Ebony And Ivory' (Paul McCartney and Stevie Wonder)

   b. 'Black Man Ray' (China Crisis)

   c. 'Black Stations White Stations' (M + M)

10. **Which 'timeless' singer duetted with choirboy Paul Miles-Kingston on the No. 3 hit 'Pie Jesu' in 1985?**

    a. Daniel O'Donnell   b. Michael Bolton   c. Sarah Brightman

For answers see p281

 **1988**

1. **What was the third Top 10 hit by Bros?**

               a. 'Drop The Boy'   *b.* 'I Owe You Nothing'

                            c. 'When Will I Be Famous?'

2. **The Fat Boys teamed up with whom on their update of 'The Twist'?**

    a. Heavy D   *b.* Big Daddy Kane   *c.* Chubby Checker

3. **Which group had hit-maker Belinda Carlisle been a member of?**

    a. Bananarama   *b.* The Go-Gos   *c.* The Bangles

4. **Name the first Debbie Gibson single to reach the Top 20.**

                            a. 'Shake Your Love'

                            b. 'Only In My Dreams'

                            c. 'Foolish Beat'

5. **Who had a Top 3 hit with 'Get Outta My Dreams Get Into My Car'?**

    a. Eurythmics   *b.* Billy Ocean   *c.* Gary Numan

For answers see p282

6. **The Stranglers hit 'All Day And All Of The Night' had been a hit in the '60s by which group?**

   a. The Beatles   *b.* The Who   *c.* The Kinks

7. **'Real Gone Kid' was the first Top 20 entry for which act?**

   a. Eighth Wonder   *b.* Deacon Blue   *c.* The Pasadenas

8. **Which Kylie Minogue hit had been a million-seller in the '60s?**

   a. 'I Should Be So Lucky'

   b. 'Got To Be Certain'

   c. 'The Loco-Motion'

9. **Which group do you associate Wendy James with?**

   a. Transvision Vamp   *b.* Salt-n-Pepa

   c. Everything But The Girl

10. **Who was named Best International Artist at the BRIT Awards?**

    a. Michael Jackson   *b.* Whitney Houston   *c.* Prince

For answers see p282

US ARTISTS
SINGLES

1. **'Missing You' was a Top 10 hit for which Bad English member?**

   a. John Parr   *b.* John Waite   *c.* John Mellencamp

2. **Who appeared in the film *Mad Max Beyond Thunderdome*?**

   a. Diana Ross   *b.* Cher   *c.* Tina Turner

3. **Who duetted with Michael Jackson on 'I Just Can't Stop Loving You'?**

   a. Janet Jackson   *b.* Siedah Garrett   *c.* Cyndi Lauper

4. **Whose biggest hits were duets with Janet Jackson and Mariah Carey?**

   a. Luther Vandross   *b.* Michael Jackson   *c.* Boyz II Men

5. **David Lee Roth was the vocalist with which hard rock group from California?**

   a. Eagles   *b.* Van Halen   *c.* Huey Lewis & The News

For answers see p282

6. **What was the name of Bruce Hornsby's backing band?**

   a. The Heartbreakers   *b.* The Range   *c.* The Revolution

7. **Name the song that Billy Vera & The Beaters had in the TV Series *Family Ties*?**

   a. 'From This Moment'

   b. 'At This Moment'

   c. 'Near This Moment'

8. **'I Think We're Alone Now' and 'Could've Been' were both hits for whom?**

   a. Tiffany   *b.* Debbie Gibson   *c.* Whitney Houston

9. **Who produced the 'We Are The World' single?**

   a. Michael Jackson   *b.* Lionel Richie   *c.* Quincy Jones

10. **Slash was the prominent guitarist with which band?**

   a. Aerosmith   *b.* Guns N' Roses   *c.* Whitesnake

For answers see p282

CHRISTMAS TUNES

1. **Name the Christmas single that sold more than 1,400,000 copies but failed to reach No. 1.**

    a. Wham!'s 'Last Christmas'

    b. Bing Crosby's 1985 re-issue of 'White Christmas'

    c. Mel and Kim's 'Rockin' Around The Christmas Tree'

2. **Which of these abusive names does *not* appear in 'Fairytale Of New York'?**

    a. Maggot   *b.* Faggot   *c.* Parrot

3. **David Bowie is reported to have said 'I hate this song. Is there something else I could sing?' about which 1982 hit?**

    a. 'Little Drummer Boy'

    b. 'I Believe In Father Christmas'

    c. 'Stop The Cavalry'

4. **'Cold As Christmas (In The Middle Of The Year)' was a minor hit for which bespectacled vocalist?**

    a. John Lennon   *b.* Elvis Costello   *c.* Elton John

5. **In which film did Welsh soprano Aled Jones's 'Walking In The Air' appear?**

    a. A Christmas Carol   *b.* Santa Claus   *c.* The Snowman

For answers see p282

6. The prolific Nat 'King' Cole appeared only once in the singles chart in the '80s. Name the re-issue that took him to No. 4 at Christmas 1987?

a. 'Unforgettable'

b. 'The Christmas Song'

c. 'When I Fall In Love'

7. What was the Christmas No. 1 in 1983?

a. Paul McCartney's 'Pipes Of Peace'

b. Billy Joel's 'Uptown Girl'

c. The Flying Pickets' 'Only You'

8. Only one act whose name includes the word 'Christmas' has charted in the UK. Can you name the group in question?

a. Santa Claus & The Christmas Trees

b. The Christmas Puddings

c. Mr Christmas & The Mince Pies

9. Where did Run-DMC spend their Christmas in 1987?

a. Hollis   b. Jail   c. Run's house

10. The festive favourite 'Santa Claus Is Comin' To Town' charted in the '70s, '80s and '90s. Who made No. 9 in 1985?

a. Bruce Springsteen   b. Carpenters   c. The Jackson Five

For answers see p282

US ARTISTS
ALBUMS

1. **Kenny Loggins sang the title track to which 1984 soundtrack album?**

    a. Flashdance   *b. Chariots Of Fire*   *c. Footloose*

2. **What was Michael Jackson's follow-up album to *Thriller*?**

    a. Off The Wall   *b. Bad*   *c. Dangerous*

3. ***Hotter Than July* is a classic album from which solo artist?**

    a. Stevie Wonder   *b.* Donna Summer

    c. Michael McDonald

4. **Who released a triple album called *Live 1975–1985*?**

    a. Bruce Springsteen   *b.* Huey Lewis & The News   *c.* Prince

5. **What was Madonna's debut album called?**

    a. True Blue   *b. Like A Prayer*   *c. Madonna*

For answers see p283

6. Complete the title of this Billy Joel album: *Songs In The* _____?

a. Attic   b. Garage   c. Kitchen

7. 'Jump' was taken from which Van Halen album?

a. 1984   b. 1985   c. 1986

8. Whose albums include *Parade* and *Around The World In A Day*?

a. Heart   b. Richard Marx   c. Prince

9. From which soundtrack is the song 'Neutron Dance' taken?

a. Beverly Hills Cop   b. Back To The Future   c. St Elmo's Fire

10. *Escape* was a Top 40 album for which band?

a. Foreigner   b. Journey   c. Chicago

For answers see p283

1989

1. **Which group did Mike & The Mechanics' Mike Rutherford also record with?**

   a. Pet Shop Boys   *b.* Simple Minds   *c.* Genesis

2. **Complete the Phil Collins title: 'Another Day In _____'.**

   a. Bed   *b.* Debt   *c.* Paradise

3. **Paul McCartney, The Christians and Holly Johnson sang together on which charity No. 1?**

   a. 'With A Little Help From My Friends'

   b. 'Let It Be'   *c.* 'Ferry 'Cross The Mersey'

4. **Edem Ephraim and Dennis Fuller were which successful act?**

   a. Milli Vanilli   *b.* London Boys   *c.* Inner City

5. **In 1989, *Top Of The Pops* celebrated what?**

   a. Its 30th birthday   *b.* Its 25th birthday   *c.* Its 1,000th show

For answers see p283

6. **Hit-makers Pat & Mick were better known as what?**

    a. Footballers   *b.* Radio DJs   *c.* Rugby players

7. **Who took a 'Homely Girl' into the Top 10 this year?**

    a. The Chi-Lites   *b.* UB40   *c.* Fine Young Cannibals

8. **Who won the BRIT Award for Best International Female Artist?**

    a. Kylie Minogue   *b.* Whitney Houston   *c.* Tracy Chapman

9. **Let's hope you don't agree with this 1989 New Model Army single when you assess this quiz!**

    a. 'Stupid Questions'

    b. 'Pathetic Questions'

    c. 'Diabolical Questions'

10. **'Beat Dis' was a big hit by which club act?**

    a. Bomb The Bass   *b.* S'Express   *c.* Coldcut

For answers see p283

1983 ALBUMS

1. **Bonnie Tyler's most popular album was called *Faster Than* _____.**

   a. *A Speeding Bullet*

   b. *Rat Up A Drain Pipe*

   c. *The Speed Of Sound*

2. **What was the title of the album that spent 37 weeks at No. 1 in the US?**

   a. *Synchronicity* – The Police

   b. *Flashdance* (soundtrack)

   c. *Thriller* – Michael Jackson

3. **Spandau Ballet's No. 1 single 'True' came from which of their albums?**

   a. *Gold*   b. *True*   c. *Ballet Favourites*

4. **Led Zeppelin's only album of the decade gave them their 10th successive gold disc. Name it.**

   a. *In Through The Out Door*   b. *Coda*

   c. *The Song Remains The Same*

5. ***The Luxury Gap* was the only Top 10 album by which act?**

   a. Japan   b. Heaven 17   c. Eurythmics

For answers see p283

6. Name the very successful series of compilation albums that started this year.

> *a.* Hits
>
> *b.* Now That's What I Call Music!
>
> *c.* Top Of The Pops

7. Complete the title of this Pink Floyd album: *The Final _____*.

> *a. Score*   *b. Album*   *c. Cut*

8. Which album broke the US chart longevity record with 491 weeks on the *Billboard* Top 200?

> *a. Sgt Pepper's Lonely Hearts Club Band* – The Beatles
>
> *b. Bat Out Of Hell* – Meat Loaf
>
> *c. Dark Side Of The Moon* – Pink Floyd

9. Who took *The Crossing* into the Top 3?

> *a.* Big Country   *b.* Christopher Cross   *c.* Level 42

10. *No Parlez* was a chart-topping debut album by which act?

> *a.* Paul Young   *b.* Tears For Fears   *c.* New Order

For answers see p283

 **1980**

1. **'I Hear You Now' was the only Top 10 hit by which act?**

   a. The Lambrettas   *b.* Jon & Vangelis   *c.* The Piranhas

2. **Who sang with Donny Hathaway on the Top 3 hit 'Back Together Again'?**

   a. Aretha Franklin   *b.* Regina Belle   *c.* Roberta Flack

3. **Which 1980 hit-maker charted with 'Tribute To Buddy Holly' in 1961?**

   a. Alvin Stardust   *b.* Mike Berry   *c.* Shakin' Stevens

4. **'Dance Yourself Dizzy' was the first Top 20 hit by which group?**

   a. Liquid Gold   *b.* Fern Kinney   *c.* The Gap Band

5. **Two of these are names of acts that had Top 20 hits in 1980 – which one is not?**

   a. Young & Co.   *b.* Coffee   *c.* Martha & The Waves

For answers see p284

6. Which act had its last Top 20 hit with 'Let's Hang On'?

a. The Four Seasons   b. The Darts   c. The Detroit Spinners

7. What was Bad Manners' first Top 20 entry called?

a. 'Lip Up Fatty'   b. 'Special Brew'   c. 'Can Can'

8. Complete the name of this group: Crown Heights
_____.

a. Crew   b. Express   c. Affair

9. Air Supply had only one UK Top 20 entry. Name it.

a. 'Even The Nights Are Better'

b. 'All Out Of Love'   c. 'Lost In Love'

10. Name the group who had a Top 10 hit with 'Amigo'.

a. Aswad   b. Light Of The World   c. Black Slate

For answers see p284

NO. 1 SINGLES

1. **Name Sister Sledge's only chart-topper.**

   a. 'We Are Family'   b. 'Lost In Music'   c. 'Frankie'

2. **Name the only US-formed group to top the UK chart in the '70s and '80s.**

   a. Blondie   b. KC & The Sunshine Band

   c. The Village People

3. **Who was Dexy's Midnight Runners' No. 1 'Geno' about?**

   a. Gene Pitney   b. Geno Washington   c. Gene Vincent

4. **Captain Sensible's No. 1 'Happy Talk' came from what musical show?**

   a. South Pacific   b. The King & I   c. My Fair Lady

5. **A Hollies hit from the 1960s returned to top the chart in the '80s. Name it.**

   a. 'The Air That I Breathe'   b. 'I'm Alive'

   c. 'He Ain't Heavy, He's My Brother'

For answers see p284

6. **What is the real name of chart-topper Adam Ant?**

   a. Anthony Adams   *b.* Adam Anthony   *c.* Stuart Goddard

7. **Complete the name of this chart-topping act: _____ & Renato.**

   a. Ronald   *b.* Ronnie   *c.* Renée

8. **Who was the only vocalist to perform on both 'Do They Know It's Christmas?' and 'We Are The World'?**

   a. Michael Jackson   *b.* Bob Geldof   *c.* Lionel Richie

9. **Which group had chart-topper Jim Diamond previously had a Top 3 hit with?**

   a. PhD   *b.* Opus   *c.* Landscape

10. **What was Stevie Wonder's first solo No. 1?**

   a. 'I Just Called To Say I Love You'

   b. 'Master Blaster'   *c.* 'Lately'

For answers see p284

MATCH THE GROUPS AND THEIR TOP 10 HITS

1. **China Crisis**

2. **Erasure**

3. **The Assembly**

4. **A Flock Of Seagulls**

5. **Chicago**

6. **Arcadia**

7. **Heart**

8. **The Beatles**

9. **Hot Chocolate**

10. **The Beautiful South**

'Hard Habit To Break'   'It Started With A Kiss'

'Love Me Do'   'Drama!'   'Never Never'   'Alone'

'Wishful Thinking'   'Wishing (If I Had A Photograph Of You)'

'Election Day'   'Song For Whoever'

For answers see p284

ROCK SINGLES

1. **Who were 'Working For The Yankee Dollar' in 1980?**

    a. The Clash   *b.* The Jam   *c.* The Skids

2. **How long were Rainbow singing for in 1980?**

    a. 'All Night Long'   *b.* 'Through Till Dawn'   *c.* 'For A Lifetime'

3. **In 1980, Saxon's wheels were made of what?**

    a. Rubber   *b.* Steel   *c.* Fire

4. **Alice Cooper warned about which dangerous substance?**

    a. 'Poison'   *b.* 'Asbestos'   *c.* 'Acid'

5. **What did Guns N' Roses recommend back in 1989?**

    a. 'Patience'   *b.* 'Canasta'   *c.* 'Rummy'

6. **What were Judas Priest breaking in 1980?**

    a. Windows   *b.* The Speed Limit   *c.* The Law

7. **According to Midnight Oil, what were burning in 1989?**

    a. Beds   *b.* Bras   *c.* Candles

8. **With which legend did U2 sing 'When Love Comes To Town' in 1989?**

    a. Bob Marley   *b.* BB King   *c.* Elvis Presley

For answers see p285

9. **What type of 'Love Missile' were Sigue Sigue Sputnik singing about in 1986?**

a. 'Love Missile F1-11'

b. 'Love Missile C3P0'

c. 'Love Missile A101'

10. **What did Def Leppard want poured on them back in 1987?**

a. Sugar   b. Gasoline   c. Treacle

For answers see p285

1981

1. In this year who heard 'Wedding Bells'?

    a. Haircut 100   b. Dire Straits   c. Godley & Creme

2. Which Rolling Stone had a Top 20 single in his own right in 1981?

    a. Mick Jagger   b. Keith Richard   c. Bill Wyman

3. Who played 'Night Games' in 1981?

    a. Saxon   b. Neil Diamond   c. Graham Bonnet

4. Complete this Fun Boy Three title: 'The _____ (Have Taken Over The Asylum)'.

    a. Lunatics   b. Fun Boy Three   c. Asylum Seekers

5. What did Altered Images wish us?

    a. 'All The Best'   b. 'Good Luck'   c. 'Happy Birthday'

6. Which of these old favourites was not returned to the Top 20 by Dave Stewart?

    a. 'What Becomes Of The Broken Hearted'

    b. '(Do) The Hucklebuck'   c. 'It's My Party'

7. 'Let's Groove' was the final Top 20 entry for which group?

    a. Ottawan   b. Earth, Wind & Fire   c. Heatwave

8. John Rocca fronted which popular club act?

    a. Freeez   b. Landscape   c. Imagination

For answers see p285

9. An offshoot of Talking Heads had a Top 10 entry with 'Wordy Rappinghood'. Name them.

    a. The Evasions   *b.* Tom Tom Club   *c.* Hi-Gloss

10. 'Einstein A Go-Go' was the unusually titled debut hit of which act?

    a. Landscape   *b.* Spandau Ballet   *c.* Modern Romance

For answers see p285

MATCH THE GROUP MEMBER WITH THEIR GROUP

1. Francis Rossi

2. John Williams

3. Pat Sharp

4. Bobby Brown

5. Donnie Wahlberg

6. Mark Moore

7. Jill Saward

8. Joseph Simmons

9. Shirley Holliman

10. Glenn Tilbrook

Shakatak   S'Express   Status Quo   Run-DMC

Squeeze   Pat & Mick   New Edition   Sky

New Kids On The Block   Pepsi & Shirlie

For answers see p285

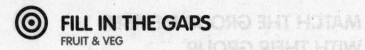

FILL IN THE GAPS
FRUIT & VEG

1. 'Every Loser Wins' (Nick _____)

2. 'Big _____' (Kajagoogoo)

3. '_____ Republic' (The Boomtown Rats)

4. '_____ Crush' (R.E.M.)

5. 'I Heard It Through The _____vine' (Marvin Gaye)

6. 'The Real Thing' (Jelly _____)

7. 'Stool Pigeon' (Kid Creole & The _____s)

8. 'Buffalo Stance' (Neneh _____)

9. 'Green _____s' (Booker T & The MGs)

10. 'Going Back To My _____s' (Odyssey)

Banana Onion Cherry Berry

Bean Root Orange Coconut

Apple Grape

For answers see p286

MATCH THE GROUP MEMBER WITH THEIR GROUP

1. Ali Campbell

2. Chris Amoo

3. Bernie Nolan

4. Ollie Brown

5. John Deacon

6. Cheryl James

7. Marcella Levy

8. Tony Hadley

9. Andrew Ridgeley

10. Martha Wash

The Weather Girls   Queen   Shakespears Sister

Spandau Ballet   Salt-n-Pepa   The Real Thing

UB40   The Nolans   Ollie & Jerry   Wham!

For answers see p286

GUESS THE SONG

1. Which item of stationery did The Beautiful South refer to in 'Song For Whoever'?

   a. Pencil case   *b.* Ruler   *c.* Compass

2. The 1988 debut single from Milli Vanilli was called what?

   a. 'Girl You Know It's True'

   b. 'Girls, We're Rob and Fabrice'

   c. 'Girl You Know We're Not Really Singing On This Record'

3. Which Chris Rea song had to be re-recorded to get it into the Top 20 in the summer of 1988?

   a. 'On The Beach'

   b. 'Fool (If You Think It's Over)'

   c. 'I Can Hear Your Heartbeat'

4. Who was 'dancing on the sand' in 1982?

   a. Belinda Carlisle   *b.* 'Rio'

   c. Florian Cloud de Bounevialle Armstrong (aka Dido)

5. According to Elvis Costello, 1981 was a good year for which flower?

   a. Daffodil   *b.* Rose   *c.* Pansy

For answers see p286

6. **Mike Peters's Alarm made their chart bow in 1983 with which numerical hit?**

   a. '68 Guns'   b. '5 Guns'   c. '100 Guns'

7. **What was German outfit Trio's repetitive No. 2 hit called?**

   a. 'Da Da Da'   b. 'Mmm Mmm Mmm'   c. 'Da Ba Dee'

8. **Complete the title of this Odyssey hit: 'Going Back To _____'.**

   a. The Future   b. New Orleans   c. My Roots

9. **What was the biggest-selling single of 1987?**

   a. 'A Good Heart'

   b. 'Never Gonna Give You Up'

   c. 'Pump Up The Jam'

10. **Name Lindsey Buckingham's sole Top 40 single away from Fleetwood Mac.**

   a. 'Little Dreamer'   b. 'Trouble'   c. 'Rooms On Fire'

For answers see p286

MATCH THE GROUPS AND THEIR TOP 10 HITS

1. Big Fun

2. The Commodores

3. ABC

4. BVSMP

5. Iron Maiden

6. Bad Manners

7. The Human League

8. Adam & The Ants

9. Go West

10. Blancmange

'Can't Shake The Feeling'   'Poison Arrow'

'I Need You'   'Ant Rap'   'Blind Vision'   'Human'

'Special Brew'   'We Close Our Eyes'   'Nightshift'

'Can I Play With Madness'

For answers see p287

1982

1. **According to the Goombay Dance Band, how many tears had flown into the river of their 1982 No. 1?**

   a. Eleven   *b.* Seven   *c.* Too Many

2. **Who was 'Girl Crazy', according to the title of a Top 10 hit from this year?**

   a. Billy Ocean   *b.* Hot Chocolate   *c.* Shakin' Stevens

3. **What was the first Top 20 entry by Wham!?**

   a. 'Wham Rap!'   *b.* 'Bad Boys'   *c.* 'Young Guns (Go For It)'

4. **'Senses Working Overtime' was the last Top 20 hit for which act?**

   a. XTC   *b.* The Pinkees   *c.* The Mobiles

5. **Which duo appeared on *Top Of The Pops* dressed as leprechauns?**

   a. Foster & Allen   *b.* Soft Cell   *c.* Pet Shop Boys

6. **Who found '(Sexual) Healing' this year?**

   a. George Michael   *b.* Barry White   *c.* Marvin Gaye

For answers see p287

7. **What OMD song was Germany's biggest-selling single this year?**

   a. 'Locomotion'

   b. 'Maid Of Orleans (The Waltz Joan Of Arc)'

   c. 'Enola Gay'

8. **What song was double A-sided with 'Town Called Malice'?**

   a. 'Eton Rifles'   *b.* 'Start'   *c.* 'Precious'

9. **Which female singer was an uncredited vocalist on Meat Loaf's 'Dead Ringer For Love'?**

   a. Cher   *b.* Diana Ross   *c.* Suzi Quatro

10. **Manager Sharon Arden married her client. Name him.**

    a. Meat Loaf   *b.* Axl Rose   *c.* Ozzy Osbourne

For answers see p287

THE CLASH

1. '_____ robber'

   a. Bank   *b.* House   *c.* Supermarket

2. 'The _____ Up'

   a. Call   *b.* Wind   *c.* Hold

3. 'Hitsville _____'

   a. UK   *b.* USA   *c.* Motown

4. 'The Magnificent _____'

   a. Eleven   *b.* Five   *c.* Seven

5. 'Should I _____ Or Should I _____'

   a. Go / Stay   *b.* Come / Leave   *c.* Stay / Go

6. 'This Is _____'

   a. London   *b.* England   *c.* Hammersmith Palais

7. '_____ Advice'

   a. Brixton   *b.* Tooting   *c.* Kingston

8. 'I Fought The _____'

   a. Cops   *b.* Law   *c.* System

9. 'Death Is A _____'

   a. Star   *b.* Choice   *c.* Certainty

10. 'Straight To _____'

   a. Hell   *b.* Bed   *c.* Bognor Regis

For answers see p287

GIRL POWER
SINGLES

1. **All About Eve's 1988 *Top Of The Pops* performance was beset by technical problems. Which track was Julianne Regan attempting to sing?**

   a. 'I Don't Want To Talk About It'

   b. 'Surrender'

   c. 'Martha's Harbour'

2. **Which appropriately named vocalist made up one half of The Weather Girls?**

   a. Kimberley Storm   b. Beverley Shower   c. Martha Wash

3. **Diane Sealey, aka Dee C. Lee, was married to which musician in the '80s?**

   a. Paul Weller   b. Freddie Mercury   c. Frank Sinatra

4. **Sonia played the girlfriend of Billy Boswell in which TV sitcom before launching her music career?**

   a. The Young Ones   b. Red Dwarf   c. Bread

5. **Who was a 'Heartbreaker' in 1982?**

   a. Dionne Warwick   b. Kiki Dee   c. Olivia Newton-John

For answers see p288

6. **Diana Ross teamed up with which singer/songwriter for the 1981 ballad 'Endless Love'?**

   a. Julio Iglesias   *b.* Lionel Richie   *c.* Smokey Robinson

7. **What surname is shared by sisters Anita, June and Ruth?**

   a. Pointer   *b.* Nolan   *c.* Jackson

8. **Annie Lennox launched her solo career with a duet featuring which soul legend?**

   a. Al Green   *b.* Luther Vandross   *c.* Alexander O'Neal

9. **'Machine just got upset' on which day, according to Hazel O'Connor?**

   a. 'Eighth Day'   *b.* 'Ninth Day'   *c.* 'Fortieth Day'

10. **Chrissie Hynde teamed up with UB40 for 'I Got You Babe' in 1985 and which other Top 10 hit in 1988?**

    a. 'Breakfast In Bed'   *b.* 'Late Lunch'

    c. 'Dinner With Gershwin'

For answers see p288

U2

1. **'When Love Comes To _____'**

   a. County Down   b. Town   c. Dublin

2. **_____ (album)**

   a. October   b. November   c. December

3. **'_____ (In The Name Of Love)'**

   a. Gloria   b. Fire   c. Pride

4. **Wide Awake In _____ (album)**

   a. America   b. The USA   c. The States

5. **'All I Want Is _____'**

   a. You   b. Everything   c. Here

6. **'Angel Of _____'**

   a. The Morning   b. Mine   c. Harlem

7. **The _____ Tree (album)**

   a. Joshua   b. Oak   c. Seventh

8. **'In _____ Country'**

   a. The   b. God's   c. Another

9. **'Two Hearts Beat _____'**

   a. Alone   b. Faster   c. As One

10. **Live – Under A _____ _____ Sky (album)**

    a. Partially Cloudy   b. Blood Red   c. Perfectly Blue

For answers see p288

FILL IN THE GAPS
DAYS AND MONTHS

1. 'January _____' (Barbara Dickson)

2. '_____ On My Mind' (Gary Moore)

3. '_____ Will Be Magic Again' (Kate Bush)

4. 'Everyday Is Like _____' (Morrissey)

5. '_____ Love' (Cherelle with Alexander O'Neal)

6. '_____ Sunshine' (The Questions)

7. 'Star Fleet' (Brian _____ & Friends)

8. '_____ Week' (The Undertones)

9. '_____ Skies' (The Jesus & Mary Chain)

10. '_____ Song' (Ian McCulloch)

Tuesday Wednesday Friday Saturday

Sunday February April May

September December

For answers see p288

GIRL POWER
SINGLES

1. **Which track was the first of Blondie's three consecutive No. 1s at the start of the '80s?**

   a. 'The Tide Is High'   b. 'Call Me'   c. 'Atomic'

2. **Mary Sandeman, aka Aneka, sang about a boy from which country in 1981?**

   a. Japan   b. China   c. Russia

3. **Where did songwriter Denise Rich dream up the Sister Sledge song 'Frankie'?**

   a. At a Frankie Goes To Hollywood concert

   b. On safari in Kenya

   c. On a flight from the US to Switzerland

4. **Our lips are sealed when it comes to her name, but we can tell you this heavenly vocalist was born in August 1958. Who is she?**

   a. Carol Decker   b. Belinda Carlisle   c. Susanna Hoffs

5. **Kylie Minogue rose to fame playing Charlene Mitchell in which Australian soap opera?**

   a. Home And Away

   b. Sons And Daughters

   c. Neighbours

For answers see p289

6. **What was the stage name of Jacqueline McKinnon, who scored a No. 1 single in 1980?**

   a. Jay Aston (Bucks Fizz)   b. Kelly Marie   c. Lena Martell

7. **Just one of Madonna's first 36 single releases failed to reach the Top 10. Can you name it?**

   a. 'Dear Jessie' (1989)   b. 'Lucky Star' (1984)

   c. 'The Look Of Love' (1987)

8. **For which sporting event did Whitney Houston record 'One Moment In Time'?**

   a. Summer Olympic Games in Seoul, 1988

   b. Football World Cup in Mexico, 1986

   c. Super Bowl XXIII in Miami, 1989

9. **Who had a 'Perfect' record as lead singer of Fairground Attraction?**

   a. Sinead O'Connor   b. Sharleen Spiteri   c. Eddi Reader

10. **Which South American river shares its name with Enya's 1988 chart-topper?**

   a. Nile   b. Orinoco   c. Rio Grande

For answers see p289

1984 ALBUMS

1. **Which UK act had their first hit album with *Café Bleu*?**

   a. The Style Council

   b. Phil Fearon & Galaxy

   c. Blancmange

2. **Which album spent 24 weeks at No. 1 in the US?**

   a. *Born In The USA* – Bruce Springsteen

   b. *Purple Rain* – Prince

   c. *Footloose* (soundtrack)

3. **Name the biggest-selling reggae album of all time, a No. 1 in 1984.**

   a. *Desmond Dekker's Greatest Hits*

   b. *The Best Of Johnny Nash*

   c. *Legend – The Best Of Bob Marley & The Wailers*

4. **Who named their chart-topping debut album *Alf*?**

   a. Howard Jones   *b.* Alison Moyet   *c.* Simple Minds

5. **What was the title of the album that introduced us to Sade?**

   a. *Diamond Life*   *b.* *Stronger Than Pride*   *c.* *Promise*

For answers see p289

6. *Waking Up With The House On Fire* was a hit album by which act?

    a. Culture Club   *b.* Marillion   *c.* Nik Kershaw

7. Which American act had their debut Top 10 album with *Break Out*?

    a. Tina Turner   *b.* The Pointer Sisters   *c.* Dio

8. Complete this Bronski Beat album title: *The Age Of* _____.

    a. Aquarius   *b.* Reasoning   *c.* Consent

9. The soundtrack album to the film *The Woman In Red* featured which act?

    a. Chris De Burgh   *b.* Stevie Wonder   *c.* Elton John

10. Who gave us *The Works* this year?

    a. David Bowie   *b.* Queen   *c.* The Smiths

For answers see p289

FILL IN THE GAPS
THE FAMILY

1. 'The Kids Are Back' (Twisted _____)

2. '_____ Figure' (George Michael)

3. 'The Harder I Try' (_____ Beyond)

4. '_____s Talk' (Tears For Fears)

5. 'Annie, I'm Not Your _____' (Kid Creole & The Coconuts)

6. '_____ Sam' (Madness)

7. 'European _____' (Japan)

8. 'Lock Up Your _____s' (Slade)

9. 'There's No One Quite Like _____' (St Winifred's School Choir)

10. '_____'s Party' (Monie Love)

Grandpa   Mother   Sister   Uncle

Father   Brother   Son   Grandma

Daddy   Daughter

For answers see p289

1983

1. **What kind of girl did New Edition sing about in their 1983 No. 1 hit?**

    a. 'Candy Girl'   *b.* 'Ballerina Girl'   *c.* 'Sexy Girl'

2. **Where were Dire Straits twisting according to their Top 20 hit of February 1983?**

    a. In The Disco   *b.* By The Pool   *c.* At The Hop

3. **Complete the title of this Bucks Fizz hit: 'When We Were _____'.**

    a. Successful   *b.* In Love   *c.* Young

4. **JoBoxers had two Top 20 entries. One was 'Boxer Beat', name the other.**

    a. 'Johnny Friendly'

    b. 'Waiting For A Train'

    c. 'Just Got Lucky'

5. **What other name did Elvis Costello have a hit with this year?**

    a. Pretender   *b.* Faker   *c.* Imposter

6. **Who had their last Top 20 entry with 'Don't Talk To Me About Love'?**

    a. Altered Images   *b.* The Belle Stars   *c.* Bucks Fizz

For answers see p290

7. 'Heartache Avenue' was the only Top 20 entry for which act?

   a. Ryan Paris   b. The Maisonettes   c. Flash & The Pan

8. At the Grammy Awards in February, which of these acts picked up a record five trophies?

   a. Christopher Cross   b. Michael Jackson   c. Toto

9. What was the correct name of the 'It's Over' hit-makers?

   a. The Funky Masters   b. The Funk Masters

   c. The Masters Of Funk

10. Name the Kajagoogoo member who successfully went solo.

   a. Paul Young   b. Limahl   c. Joe Jackson

For answers see p290

NO. 1 ALBUMS

1. **John Lennon & Yoko Ono's 1981 chart-topper was _____?**

   a. Fantasy   *b.* Double Fantasy   *c.* Treble Fantasy

2. ***Turn Back The Clock* was a No. 1 in 1988 by which group?**

   a. Johnny Hates Jazz   *b.* Glenn Medeiros   *c.* S-Express

3. **Who told *The Whole Story* in 1987?**

   a. Simple Minds   *b.* Suzanne Vega   *c.* Kate Bush

4. **Which of these was *not* a No. 1 album for Madonna?**

   a. Like A Prayer   *b.* The First Album   *c.* Like A Virgin

5. **What is the real name of chart-topper Meat Loaf?**

   a. Larry Lee Loafelli   *b.* Marvin Lee Aday

   c. John Lee Montgomery

6. **Complete the name of the chart-topping Aussie band: Men At _____.**

   a. Play   *b.* Home   *c.* Work

7. **The album *Peter Gabriel* was a No. 1 in 1980. How many other albums did he release with that same title?**

   a. 3   *b.* 2   *c.* 1

8. **Which US R&B act's *Greatest Hits* topped the chart in 1980?**

   a. Rose Royce   *b.* Odyssey   *c.* George Benson

For answers see p290

9. **Who had a chart-topping *Foreign Affair* in 1989?**

    a. Tanita Tikaram   *b.* Tina Turner   *c.* Bobby Brown

10. **Complete Paul Young's chart-topping album title: *The Secret Of* _____.**

    a. Love   *b.* Success   *c.* Association

For answers see p290

DUETS

1. **The vocal talents of Sarah Jane Morris can be heard on which '80s track?**

   a. 'All I Ask Of You'   *b.* 'She's Leaving Home'

   c. 'Don't Leave Me This Way'

2. **Linda Ronstadt was 'Somewhere Out There' with which singer?**

   a. Narada Michael Walden

   b. James Ingram

   c. George Benson

3. **Which Shadow joined the mayhem when Cliff Richard and The Young Ones re-recorded 'Living Doll' in 1986?**

   a. Bruce Welch   *b.* Hank B. Marvin   *c.* Tony Meehan

4. **Grandmaster Flash teamed up with which vocalist on 'White Lines (Don't Don't Do It)'?**

   a. Smellie Mellie   *b.* Melle Mel   *c.* Mellie Vanelli

5. **What had Kylie and Jason done in *Neighbours* three weeks before the release of 'Especially For You'?**

   a. Got married   *b.* Filed for divorce   *c.* Been killed off

6. **Name the Top 10 duet that coaxed Dusty Springfield out of her Californian exile in 1987.**

   a. 'What Have I Done To Deserve This?'   *b.* 'In Private'

   c. 'Nothing Has Been Proved'

For answers see p290

7. 'I Got You Babe' (UB40 featuring Chrissie Hynde) and 'Dancing In The Street' (David Bowie and Mick Jagger) were back-to-back No. 1s in which year?

    a. 1981   *b.* 1985   *c.* 1989

8. Which duet can be found on the 1983 album *Eyes That Can See In The Dark*?

    a. 'Sisters Are Doin' It For Themselves'

    b. 'Islands In The Stream'   *c.* 'The Arms Of Orion'

9. How many years separated the release of Gene Pitney's original version of 'Something's Gotten Hold Of My Heart' and his No. 1 duet with Marc Almond?

    a. 21 years   *b.* 13 years   *c.* 32 years

10. Whose 1987 performance of 'Diamond Lights' on *Top Of The Pops* was described as 'Four left feet, two mullets and a pair of ventriloquist dummies in bad suits'?

    a. Glenn Hoddle and Chris Waddle

    b. Kevin Keegan and ventriloquist dummy

    c. John Barnes and Keith Allen

For answers see p290

BUCKS FIZZ

1.   '_____ Your _____ Up'
   a. Waking / Wife   b. Making / Mind   c. Lifting / Arms

2.   'Piece Of The _____'
   a. Action   b. Cake   c. Jigsaw

3.   'One Of Those _____'
   a. Days   b. Nights   c. Things

4.   'My _____ Never Lies'
   a. Wallet   b. iPod   c. Camera

5.   *Are You _____?* (album)
   a. Experienced   b. Happy   c. Ready

6.   'If You Can't Stand The _____'
   a. Heat   b. Beat   c. Meat

7.   '_____ Town'
   a. Camden   b. London   c. China

8.   '_____ In Your Sleep'
   a. Talking   b. Walking   c. Snoring

9.   'You And Your _____ So _____'
   a. Love / Real   b. Girl / Happy   c. Heart / Blue

10.   'New Beginning (_____)'
   a. Mumbai Venture   b. Mamba Seyra   c. Mambo Italiano

For answers see p291

 **DUETS**

1. **With whom did Julio Iglesias share the vocals on the song 'To All The Girls I've Loved Before' in 1984?**

   a. Willie Nelson   *b.* Donnie Wahlberg   *c.* Peter Cetera

2. **With whom did Elaine Paige duet on the 1985 No. 1 hit 'I Know Him So Well'?**

   a. Barbara Dickson

   b. Barbara Windsor

   c. Barbra Streisand

3. **With whom did George Michael duet on the 1987 No. 1 hit 'I Knew You Were Waiting (For Me)'?**

   a. Aretha Franklin   *b.* Sinitta   *c.* Carly Simon

4. **With whom did Sarah Brightman duet on the 1986 Top 10 hit 'The Phantom Of The Opera'?**

   a. Cliff Richard   *b.* Steve Harley   *c.* Michael Crawford

5. **Who duetted with Phil Collins on 'Separate Lives' in 1985?**

   a. Marilyn Martin   *b.* Syreeta   *c.* David Crosby

For answers see p291

6.   **Who duetted with Tina Turner on 'It's Only Love' in 1985?**

   a. Jimmy Somerville   *b.* Bryan Adams   *c.* Neil Tennant

7.   **With whom did Stevie Wonder record the minor 1988 single 'Get It'?**

   a. Smokey Robinson   *b.* Michael Jackson   *c.* Julio Iglesias

8.   **Where were Giorgio Moroder and Philip Oakey 'Together' in 1984?**

   a. On A Plane   *b.* In Electric Dreams   *c.* Out In The Fields

9.   **Daryl Dragon is a member of which duo?**

   a. Erasure   *b.* Captain & Tennille   *c.* Pet Shop Boys

10.   **The unusual pairing of Eartha Kitt and Bronski Beat teamed up on which moderately successful 1989 single?**

   a. 'You Make Me Feel (Mighty Real)'

   b. 'Cha Cha Heels'   *c.* 'Under The Bridges Of Paris'

For answers see p291

◎ GIRL POWER
MATCH THE LADIES AND THEIR TOP 10 HITS

1. Debbie Harry

2. Denise LaSalle

3. Donna Summer

4. Debbie Gibson

5. Evelyn Thomas

6. Deniece Williams

7. Dionne Warwick

8. Elkie Brooks

9. Diana Ross

10. Dee C. Lee

'No More The Fool'   'Foolish Beat'   'See The Day'

'Upside Down'   'High Energy'   'Let's Hear It For The Boy'

'All The Love In The World'   'This Time I Know It's For Real'

'French Kissin' In The USA'   'My Toot Toot'

For answers see p291

ORIGINATES FROM

MATCH THE TOP 10 ACT AND THE COUNTRY THEY CAME FROM

1. Montserrat Caballe

2. INXS

3. Japan

4. Joe Dolce

5. Mai Tai

6. Europe

7. Falco

8. Harold Faltermeyer

9. Nana Mouskouri

10. Desireless

France   Sweden   Austria   Australia

Spain   Germany   UK   US

Guyana   Greece

For answers see p292

1984

1. **Bronski Beat's first Top 20 hit was called what?**

   a. 'Smalltown Boy'   *b.* 'I Feel Love'   *c.* 'Why'

2. **Clare Grogan left which group this year?**

   a. Eighth Wonder   *b.* Altered Images   *c.* Bow Wow Wow

3. **Which later solo star sang on the hit 'Dr Beat'?**

   a. Madonna   *b.* Gloria Estefan   *c.* Cyndi Lauper

4. **Ex-Specials and Fun Boy Three member Terry Hall launched which new group?**

   a. Toy Dolls   *b.* The Colourfield   *c.* Hall Or Nothing

5. **Who had their only Top 20 entry with 'Break My Stride'?**

   a. Joe Fagin   *b.* Juan Martin   *c.* Matthew Wilder

For answers see p292

6. **Which politician appeared with Tracey Ullman in her 'My Guy' video?**

   a. Tony Blair   *b.* John Major   *c.* Neil Kinnock

7. **Who said 'Hello' to the No. 1 spot in 1984?**

   a. Lionel Richie   *b.* Neil Diamond   *c.* Stevie Wonder

8. **What was The Jacksons' successful comeback tour called?**

   a. The Jacksons Are Back

   b. The Return of Michael & His Brothers

   c. Victory

9. **Neil's hippie hit 'Hole In My Shoe' was first recorded by which group?**

   a. The Spencer Davis Group   *b.* Traffic   *c.* Procol Harum

10. **Where did Simple Minds' Jim Kerr marry The Pretenders' Chrissie Hynde?**

    a. In a Glasgow registry office

    b. On stage at a Pretenders gig

    c. In Central Park, New York

For answers see p292

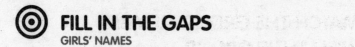

FILL IN THE GAPS
GIRLS' NAMES

1. 'Oh _____' (Shakin' Stevens)

2. 'La _____ Bonita' (Madonna)

3. '_____ Sometimes' (The Cure)

4. '_____' (Starship)

5. 'Come On _____' (Dexy's Midnight Runners)

6. 'Do Nothing' / '_____'s Farm' (The Specials)

7. 'Baby _____' (Rod Stewart)

8. '_____' (Status Quo, *Live At The NEC*)'

9. '_____' (Level 42)

10. '_____' (Cliff Richard)

Tracie   Eileen   Carrie   Charlotte

Julie   Jane   Sara   Isla

Maggie   Caroline

For answers see p292

MATCH THE GROUP MEMBER WITH THEIR GROUP

1. Ritchie Blackmore

2. Jerry Dammers

3. Joey Ramone

4. Charlie Reid

5. Jeffrey Daniel

6. Richard 'A' Hewson

7. Nellee Hooper

8. Tom Bailey

9. Marie Fredriksson

10. Kathy Sledge

The Proclaimers   Shalamar   Sister Sledge

The Rah Band   Roxette   The Specials   Rainbow

The Ramones   Soul II Soul   Thompson Twins

For answers see p293

CHRISTMAS TUNES

1. **In which year did 'Do They Know It's Christmas?' first reach the top of the charts?**

   a. 1982   b. 1984   c. 1989

2. **What is the correct title of the 1985 No. 1 by Shakin' Stevens?**

   a. 'Merry Christmas Everyone'

   b. 'Blue Christmas'   c. 'Happy Xmas Everybody'

3. **St Winifred's School Choir bagged the top spot at Christmas 1980. Who provided the ensemble's lead vocals?**

   a. Dawn Ralph   b. Claire Usher   c. Denise Van Outen

4. **The David Essex ballad 'A Winter's Tale' stalled at which number?**

   a. No. 2   b. No. 7   c. No. 21

5. **Cliff Richard's 12th chart-topper arrived in 1988. Name it.**

   a. 'Miss You Nights'   b. 'Little Town'   c. 'Mistletoe And Wine'

For answers see p293

6. **Who was 'Driving Home For Christmas' in 1988?**

   a. Chris De Burgh *b.* Chris Rea *c.* Chrissie Hynde

7. **Which indefatigable Christmas hit peaked at No. 70 in 1980, No. 32 in 1981, No. 67 in 1982, No. 20 in 1983, No. 47 in 1984, No. 48 in 1985 and No. 71 in 1986?**

   a. 'Merry Xmas Everybody'

   b. 'I Wish It Could Be Christmas Everyday'

   c. 'White Christmas'

8. **Complete the title of this Chris De Burgh song: 'A _____ Came Travelling'.**

   a. Ferryman *b.* Crusader *c.* Spaceman

9. **What Christmas-themed activity were The Waitresses doing in 1982?**

   a. Wrapping *b.* Carol-singing *c.* Eating cold turkey

10. **The Pretenders clocked up how many miles on their Christmas 1983 offering?**

    a. '2000 Miles' *b.* '500 Miles' *c.* '977 Miles'

For answers see p293

1985

1. **Which ex-Clash member launched the group Big Audio Dynamite?**

   a. Joe Strummer   b. Mick Jones   c. Nicky Headon

2. **What words in brackets form part of the title of John Parr's hit 'St Elmo's Fire'?**

   a. (Man In Motion)   b. (It's Hot, Hot, Hot)   c. (Put It Out)

3. **Who picked up the BRIT award for Best British Female?**

   a. Sade   b. Bonnie Tyler   c. Alison Moyet

4. **What was the title of Madonna's 1985 film?**

   a. Desperately Seeking Sheila

   b. Desperately Seeking Sarah

   c. Desperately Seeking Susan

5. **Who had a 'White Wedding' this year?**

   a. Howard Jones   b. Billy Idol   c. Paul Young

For answers see p293

6. Complete the name of this hit act: The _____ & Mary Chain.

a. Peter, Paul   *b.* Hairy   *c.* Jesus

7. Paul Young's 'Everytime You Go Away' was written by which of these people?

a. John Oates   *b.* Daryl Hall   *c.* Stevie Wonder

8. Model Christie Brinkley married which singer?

a. Bruce Springsteen   *b.* Billy Idol   *c.* Billy Joel

9. Who reached the Top 10 with a version of Led Zeppelin's 'Stairway To Heaven'?

a. The Muppets   *b.* The Far Corporation   *c.* Dread Zeppelin

10. Which act played ten nights at Wembley Arena?

a. Eric Clapton   *b.* Bruce Springsteen   *c.* Dire Straits

For answers see p293

POWER BALLADS

1. **Which fairytale character shares her name with the band behind 'Don't Know What You Got (Till It's Gone)'?**

   a. Cinderella   *b.* Snow White   *c.* Sleeping Beauty

2. **Where was Bryan Adams born?**

   a. Sheffield, England

   b. Auckland, New Zealand

   c. Ontario, Canada

3. **Who did Joe Cocker duet with on the 1983 Top 10 smash 'Up Where We Belong'?**

   a. Wendy Fraser   *b.* Jennifer Warnes   *c.* Barbra Streisand

4. **Complete the Poison song title: 'Every Rose Has Its _____'.**

   a. Petals   *b.* Day   *c.* Thorn

5. **What was INXS's only Top 10 single?**

   a. 'Need You Tonight'   *b.* 'Mystify'   *c.* 'Never Tear Us Apart'

For answers see p294

6. **What was Robert Palmer addicted to back in 1986?**

    a. Love   *b.* Bass   *c.* Crosswords

7. **U2's 'With Or Without You' was the lead single from which classic album, released in 1987?**

    a. War   *b.* The Joshua Tree   *c.* Zooropa

8. **What was the working title of the song that became the Queen/David Bowie collaboration 'Under Pressure'?**

    a. 'Feel Like'   *b.* 'Our Last Dance'   *c.* 'People On Streets'

9. **The Spencer Davis Group, Blind Faith, Traffic and 'Higher Love' are clues to the identity of which musician?**

    a. Steve Winwood   *b.* Peter Gabriel   *c.* Ginger Baker

10. **Which band sang 'Wanted Dead Or Alive' in 1987?**

    a. Bon Jovi   *b.* Aerosmith   *c.* Journey

For answers see p294

US ARTISTS ALBUMS

1. **Who released an eponymous debut album and a second album with the same title as her christian name?**

   a. Paula Abdul   *b.* Madonna Ciccone   *c.* Whitney Houston

2. **Which member of the Traveling Wilburys died before the release of their second album?**

   a. Tom Petty   *b.* Roy Orbison   *c.* Bob Dylan

3. **From which soundtrack is 'The Power Of Love' by Huey Lewis taken?**

   a. Back To The Future   *b.* Dirty Dancing

   c. The NeverEnding Story

4. **Which multicoloured-haired female's debut album was called *She's So Unusual*?**

   a. Pat Benatar   *b.* Cyndi Lauper   *c.* Tina Turner

5. **'Kokomo' by The Beach Boys was taken from which soundtrack album?**

   a. Cocktail   *b.* Rain Man   *c.* Top Gun

For answers see p294

6. What Bon Jovi album is named after their home state?

a. New Jersey   b. New York   c. New Hampshire

7. In what year was the album *Thriller* released?

a. 1982   b. 1985   c. 1988

8. Complete the title of the 1987 Beastie Boys album: *Licence To* _____?

a. Kill   b. Ill   c. Fill

9. Who was *Loc'ed After Dark* in 1989?

a. Run-DMC   b. Tone Loc   c. Tupac Shakur

10. What was Pat Benatar's most successful album in the UK?

a. Best Shots   b. Tropico   c. Precious Time

For answers see p294

FILL IN THE GAPS

THE WEATHER

1. 'Purple _____' (Prince & The Revolution)

2. 'All Out Of Love' (_____ Supply)

3. 'The _____ Always Shines On TV' (a-ha)

4. 'The Boys Of _____' (Don Henley)

5. 'You Have Placed A _____ In My Heart' (Euryhtmics)

6. 'All Night Long' (_____)

7. 'Pure' (The _____ Seeds)

8. 'A _____'s Tale' (David Essex)

9. 'She's Like The _____' (Patrick Swayze)

10. 'Where Were You Hiding When The _____ Broke' (The Alarm)

Air   Chill   Lightning   Rain

Rainbow   Storm   Summer   Sun

Winter   Wind

For answers see p294

1985 ALBUMS

1. *Hits Out Of Hell* was the title of an album by whom?

   a. Ozzy Ozbourne   *b.* Alice Cooper   *c.* Meat Loaf

2. Which album act arrived at the BRIT Awards surrounded by bodyguards?

   a. Madonna   *b.* Bruce Springsteen   *c.* Prince

3. Complete the title of Dire Straits' top-selling album: *Brothers In* _____.

   a. Law   *b.* Trouble   *c.* Arms

4. Which famous group vocalist had a solo Top 10 album with *She's The Boss*?

   a. Boy George   *b.* Mick Jagger   *c.* Sting

5. Which of these was the first Top 10 album for Talking Heads?

   a. True Stories   *b.* Little Creatures   *c.* Remain In Light

6. Which female singer's album *Hounds Of Love* entered the chart at No. 1?

   a. Grace Jones   *b.* Jennifer Rush   *c.* Kate Bush

7. Name the UK No. 1 album by Phil Collins that gave him his first US chart-topper.

   a. No Jacket Required

   b. Hello I Must Be Going

   c. Face Value

For answers see p295

8. Who gave us *Songs From The Big Chair*?

a. Depeche Mode   b. Elvis Costello   c. Tears For Fears

9. What was the name of the boat which almost drowned Duran Duran's Simon Le Bon this year?

a. Drum   b. Bass   c. Guitar

10. After a record run of 324 weeks, which album finally left the UK chart?

a. *Sgt Pepper's Lonely Hearts Club Band* – The Beatles

b. *Dark Side Of The Moon* – Pink Floyd

c. *Bat Out Of Hell* – Meat Loaf

For answers see p295

GIRL POWER
MATCH THE LADIES AND THEIR TOP 10 HITS

1. Fern Kinney

2. Hazell Dean

3. Janet Jackson

4. Hazel O'Connor

5. Joyce Sims

6. Gloria Estefan

7. Judy Boucher

8. Irene Cara

9. Jaki Graham

10. Gwen Guthrie

'Don't Wanna Lose You'

'Ain't Nothin' Goin' On But The Rent'

'Together We Are Beautiful'

'Searchin' (I Gotta Find A Man)'

'Can't Be With You Tonight'

'Let's Wait Awhile'

'Fame'

'Set Me Free'

'Will You'

'Come Into My Life'

For answers see p295

◎ MATCH THE GROUP MEMBER WITH THEIR GROUP

1. Curt Smith

2. Steve Strange

3. Brian Setzer

4. Kenney Jones

5. Annie Lennox

6. Midge Ure

7. David Weiss

8. Phil Lynott

9. Tina Weymouth

10. Hugh Cornwell

The Stranglers   Talking Heads   Tears For Fears

Thin Lizzy   The Tourists   Visage   The Stray Cats

Ultravox   The Who   Was (Not Was)

For answers see p295

ROCK SINGLES

1. **Which Dave Mustaine-fronted band woke up dead on their 1987 debut?**

   a. The Sisters Of Mercy   *b.* Slayer   *c.* Megadeth

2. **Other than '90s singles 'Wind Of Change' and 'Send Me An Angel', only one other Scorpions single – a double A-side – made the Top 40. Name it.**

   a. 'Is There Anybody There?' / 'Another Piece Of Meat'

   b. 'Is There Anybody In The Building?' / 'Another Cup Of Coffee'

   c. 'Is There Anybody Listening?' / 'Another Plate Of Chips'

3. **With which song did Bob Seger & The Silver Bullet Band fail to reach the Top 40 for a second time in 1982?**

   a. 'We've Got Tonite'

   b. 'Night Moves'

   c. 'Against The Wind'

4. **Identify the garment that completes this Who single: 'Don't Let Go The _____'.**

   a. Jumper   *b.* Coat   *c.* Scarf

5. **Where were 'The Final Countdown' rockers Europe from?**

   a. Sweden   *b.* Czech Republic   *c.* Poland

6. **Who were the uncredited vocalists on Run-DMC's 'Walk This Way'?**

   a. Joe Perry and Steven Tyler

   b. Jon Bon Jovi and Richie Sambora

   c. Brian May and Roger Taylor

For answers see p296

7. Who walks down the street at the start of Queen's 'Another One Bites The Dust?'

   a. Steve   *b.* Trevor   *c.* Bob

8. What price was Metallica's *Garage Days Re-Revisited* EP, according to the title?

   a. £2.99   *b.* $7,000   *c.* $5.98

9. Ritchie Blackmore re-joined which band after 'I Surrender' rockers Rainbow split up in 1984?

   a. King Crimson   *b.* Gillan   *c.* Deep Purple

10. What is the correct act billing for the single 'Layla'?

   a. Eric & The Dominos   *b.* Cream   *c.* Derek & The Dominos

For answers see p296

1986

1. **Who introduced us to their 'Brother Louie'?**

   a. Talking Heads   *b.* Modern Talking   *c.* Talk Talk

2. **Who received an honorary knighthood this year?**

   a. Cliff Richard   *b.* Mick Jagger   *c.* Bob Geldof

3. **'(I Just) Died In Your Arms' was the first and biggest hit for which act?**

   a. Hollywood Beyond   *b.* Cutting Crew   *c.* It Bites

4. **Ex-Cream drummer Ginger Baker joined which group?**

   a. PIL   *b.* The Damned   *c.* Dire Straits

5. **What was the first Top 20 single by Erasure?**

   a. 'Sometimes'   *b.* 'It Doesn't Have To Be'   *c.* 'Victim Of Love'

6. **What was the title of the film about Sid Vicious?**

   a. The Great Rock 'n' Roll Swindle

   b. Ex-Sex Pistol Story   *c.* Sid And Nancy

7. **Complete this James Brown hit title: 'Living In _____'.**

   a. Sin   *b.* Poverty   *c.* America

8. **The Damned clocked up their last Top 20 entry in 1986. What was it called?**

   a. 'Eloise'   *b.* 'Alone Again Or'   *c.* 'Anything'

For answers see p296

9. Joe Leeway left one of the regular chart groups in this year. Name them.

a. Madness   b. Culture Club   c. Thompson Twins

10. Which successful group were made up of members of the Pearson family?

a. The Housemartins   b. The Real Thing   c. Five Star

For answers see p296

FILL IN THE GAPS
THE BODY

1. 'My Simple _____' (The Three Degrees)

2. '(I Just) Died In Your _____s' (Cutting Crew)

3. '_____' (ZZ Top)

4. 'China In Your _____' (T'Pau)

5. 'Oops Upside Your _____' (The Gap Band)

6. '_____loose' (Kenny Loggins)

7. '_____ Of The Tiger' (Survivor)

8. 'A Night In New York' (_____ Bones & The Racketeers)

9. 'Wrapped Around Your _____' (The Police)

10. 'World Shut Your _____' (Julian Cope)

Head   Hand   Mouth   Heart

Arm   Legs   Foot   Finger

Elbow   Eye

For answers see p296

GUESS THE ARTIST

1. **Who had a Top 5 hit in 1980 with the double A-side 'It's Only Love' / 'Beyond The Reef'?**

   a. Elvis Presley   *b.* Tina Turner   *c.* UB40

2. **Aneka reached No. 1 in 1981 with 'Japanese Boy'. What is her real name?**

   a. Mary O'Brien   *b.* Mary Sandeman   *c.* Mary Hopkin

3. **Who had a Top 20 hit in 1981 with 'Once In A Lifetime'?**

   a. Tears For Fears   *b.* Talking Heads   *c.* Simple Minds

4. **Who made the Top 5 in October 1982 with 'Starmaker'?**

   a. Bananarama

   b. The Kids From 'Fame'

   c. Modern Romance

5. **Which 'Unforgettable' singer charted with the ballad 'Miss You Like Crazy'?**

   a. Natalie Cole   *b.* Debbie Gibson   *c.* Chaka Khan

For answers see p297

6. **Patrick Swayze had a Top 20 hit in 1988 with 'She's Like The Wind', but who was his female guest vocalist?**

   a. Lynne Hamilton   *b.* Jennifer Warnes   *c.* Wendy Fraser

7. **Enya had a 1988 chart-topper with 'Orinoco Flow'. What is her surname?**

   a. O'Connor   *b.* O'Riordan   *c.* Brennan

8. **They had the last No. 1 of the '70s and the first No. 1 of the '80s. Name them.**

   a. The Detroit Spinners   *b.* Pink Floyd

   c. Electric Light Orchestra

9. **Who was the chart-topping 'Coward Of The County' in 1980?**

   a. Johnny Cash   *b.* Glen Campbell   *c.* Kenny Rogers

10. **Mani and Reni were two members of which 'Madchester' band?**

   a. The Stone Roses   *b.* The Fall   *c.* Happy Mondays

For answers see p297

NO. 1 SINGLES

1. **Barry Manilow had a US Top 40 hit with a cover of which UK No. 1 from 1982?**

   a. 'Oh Julie' – Shakin' Stevens

   b. 'Come On Eileen' – Dexy's Midnight Runners

   c. 'The Land Of Make Believe' – Bucks Fizz

2. **Chart-topper Captain Sensible originally played in what group?**

   a. The Clash   b. The Damned   c. Sex Pistols

3. **Complete the title of this New Kids On The Block No. 1: 'You Got It (_____)'**

   a. I Want It   b. The Good Stuff   c. The Right Stuff

4. **What was ABBA's other No. 1 in the '80s apart from 'The Winner Takes It All'?**

   a. 'I Have A Dream'   b. 'Super Trouper'

   c. 'Take A Chance On Me'

5. **The Jam's 'Going Underground' was a double-sided No. 1. What was the other side called?**

   a. 'Dreams Of Children'

   b. '"A" Bomb In Wardour Street'

   c. 'Precious'

For answers see p297

6. **What was Kylie Minogue's first No. 1?**

a. 'The Loco-Motion'   b. 'Got To Be Certain'

c. 'I Should Be So Lucky'

7. **Name the act who topped the chart with 'Doctorin' The Tardis'.**

a. The Time Travellers

b. The Gallifrey Three

c. The Timelords

8. **Which of these Adam Ant No. 1s was not credited to Adam & The Ants, just Adam Ant?**

a. 'Goody Two Shoes'

b. 'Stand And Deliver'

c. 'Prince Charming'

9. **Complete the name of the group who told us to 'Shaddap You Face': Joe Dolce _____.**

a. Theatre Company   b. Music Theatre   c. Music Company

10. **How many No. 1 hits did Whitney Houston have in the '80s?**

a. 1   b. 2   c. 3

For answers see p297

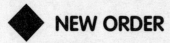 **NEW ORDER**

1. **Which member of New Order was *not* in Joy Division?**

   a. Bernard Sumner   *b.* Gillian Gilbert   *c.* Stephen Morris

2. **Fill in the blank: 'Blue Monday' is the UK's biggest-selling _____ single.**

   a. 7-inch   *b.* 12-inch   *c.* Cassette

3. **New Order made their chart debut in 1981 with which single?**

   a. 'Ceremony'   *b.* 'Confusion'   *c.* 'Crystal'

4. **Which city is home to New Order?**

   a. London   *b.* Norwich   *c.* Manchester

5. **What was the title of the band's first Top 10 album, released in 1983?**

   a. Power, Corruption And Lies   *b.* Law And Order

   c. Time, Love And Tenderness

For answers see p297

6. **Name the bass player who went on to form the band Monaco.**

   a. Stephen Morris   *b.* Bernard Sumner   *c.* Peter Hook

7. **Bernard Sumner founded Electronic in 1988 with whom?**

   a. Johnny Marr   *b.* Karl Bartos   *c.* Neil Tennant

8. **On 1 June 1982, New Order recorded a session – released as an EP in 1986 – for which DJ?**

   a. John Peel   *b.* Tommy Vance   *c.* Steve Wright

9. **What was New Order's first No. 1 album called?**

   a. Movement   *b.* Technique   *c.* Shellshock

10. **Complete the title of the band's 1981 double A-side: 'Procession' / 'Everything's Gone _____'.**

    a. Green   *b.* Black   *c.* Blue

For answers see p297

GIRL POWER

1. Nice and Greece are listed as places Charlene Duncan had travelled to, but where had she never been, according to the title of her 1982 No. 1?

   a. Me   *b.* You   *c.* Us

2. 'It's 'Orrible Being In Love (When You're 8 1/2)' hit-maker Claire shares her surname with which modern-day R&B star?

   a. Usher   *b.* Ashanti   *c.* Rihanna

3. If 20 of Nena's red balloons burst, how many would she have left, according to her 1984 hit?

   a. 79   *b.* 80   *c.* 81

4. Which country did Nicole represent at the 1982 Eurovision Song Contest with 'A Little Peace'?

   a. France   *b.* Germany   *c.* Ireland

5. Which floor-filler was a Top 10 hit twice for Chaka Khan, in 1984 and 1989?

   a. 'I'm Every Woman'   *b.* 'Ain't Nobody'   *c.* 'I Feel For You'

For answers see p298

6. **Identify Sade's correct name and country of birth?**

   a. Helen Folasade Adu, Nigeria

   b. Hilda Tloubatla, South Africa

   c. Sade Shabalala, Morocco

7. **What did one-hit wonder Phyllis Nelson request listeners to do?**

   a. 'Stay Where You Are'   *b.* 'Move Closer'   *c.* 'Get Lost'

8. **Whose vocal talents can be heard on Soul II Soul's 'Keep On Moving' and 'Back To Life (However Do You Want Me)'?**

   a. Kym Mazelle   *b.* Caron Wheeler   *c.* Rose Windross

9. **Which dance group performed on *Top Of The Pops* until 1981?**

   a. Legs & Co.   *b.* Flick Colby   *c.* WowFabGroovy

10. **Bangles bass player Michael Steele is what?**

   a. A man   *b.* A woman   *c.* Not in The Bangles

For answers see p298

1987

1. **Where did The Proclaimers hope to get a letter from?**

   a. The Tax Man   *b.* The Scottish Tourist Board   *c.* America

2. **Which group did Morrissey leave this year?**

   a. The Communards   *b.* Pet Shop Boys   *c.* The Smiths

3. **Who represented the UK in the Eurovision Song Contest?**

   a. Rikki   *b.* Vikki   *c.* Trikki

4. **Who had a 1987 Top 5 hit with 'Crockett's Theme'?**

   a. Clannad   *b.* Don Johnson   *c.* Jan Hammer

5. **Who performed with Michael Jackson on his 1987 hit 'I Just Can't Stop Loving You'?**

   a. Diana Ross   *b.* Janet Jackson   *c.* Siedah Garrett

For answers see p298

6. **What was the title of Def Leppard's first Top 20 entry?**

   a. 'Animal'

   b. 'Pour Some Sugar On Me'

   c. 'Armageddon It'

7. **Eurythmic Dave Stewart married Siobhan Fahey. Which group was she from?**

   a. Amazulu   *b.* Bananarama   *c.* Pepsi & Shirley

8. **Who took home the BRIT award for Best British Male Solo Artist?**

   a. Phil Collins   *b.* Robert Palmer   *c.* Peter Gabriel

9. **Which Island did Madonna go to?**

   a. Juanita   *b.* Bonita   *c.* Sinitti

10. **Which of the following did not sing on the Ferry Aid charity hit 'Let It Be'?**

   a. George Harrison   *b.* Boy George   *c.* Kate Bush

For answers see p298

NO. 1 SINGLES

1. **Which 1957 recording topped the chart in 1986?**
   - *a.* 'When A Man Loves A Woman' – Percy Sledge
   - *b.* 'Wonderful World' – Sam Cooke
   - *c.* 'Reet Petite (The Sweetest Girl In Town)' – Jackie Wilson

2. **Name Madonna's first No. 1.**
   - *a.* 'Like A Virgin'
   - *b.* 'Material Girl'
   - *c.* 'Into The Groove'

3. **Who wrote the Roxy Music chart-topper 'Jealous Guy'?**
   - *a.* Bryan Ferry
   - *b.* John Lennon
   - *c.* Brian Eno

4. **'Fantasy Island' was the Top 5 follow-up to which No. 1?**
   - *a.* 'The Lion Sleeps Tonight' – Tight Fit
   - *b.* 'Rock Me Amadeus' – Falco
   - *c.* 'Too Shy' – Kajagoogoo

5. **Who topped the chart with the Gibb Brothers song 'Chain Reaction'?**
   - *a.* The Bee Gees
   - *b.* Olivia Newton-John
   - *c.* Diana Ross

For answers see p298

6. Name the first No. 1 for top production team Stock, Aitken & Waterman.

a. 'You Spin Me Round (Like A Record)'

b. 'I Should Be So Lucky'   c. 'Roadblock'

7. Who plays the harmonica on the Eurythmics' 'There Must Be An Angel (Playing With My Heart)'?

a. Bob Dylan   b. Stevie Wonder   c. Rod Stewart

8. What is the real name of 'When The Going Gets Tough' hit-maker Billy Ocean?

a. Brinsley Forde   b. Leslie Charles   c. Everton Bonner

9. What did Bros owe you in 1988?

a. Money   b. Everything   c. Nothing

10. Complete the name of this chart-topping act: Yazz &
_____.

a. Yazoo   b. The Mastermixers   c. The Plastic Population

For answers see p298

ADAM & THE ANTS

1. **'Dog Eat _____'**
   - a. Dog
   - b. Food
   - c. Grass

2. **'Young _____'**
   - a. Ones
   - b. Barbarians
   - c. Parisians

3. **'Kings Of The Wild _____'**
   - a. Frontier
   - b. West
   - c. Guns

4. **'_____ And Deliver'**
   - a. Stand
   - b. Sit
   - c. Post

5. **'Prince _____'**
   - a. Witty
   - b. Delightful
   - c. Charming

6. **'_____ Girls'**
   - a. Deutscher
   - b. Croydon
   - c. Parisian

7. **'_____ Boots'**
   - a. Puss 'n
   - b. Kinky
   - c. Cowboy

8. **'Apollo _____'**
   - a. 6
   - b. 9
   - c. 11

9. **'Ant_____'**
   - a. Rap
   - b. Music
   - c. Powder

10. **Dirk Wears White _____ (album)**
    - a. Stripes
    - b. Vests
    - c. Sox

For answers see p299

LYRICS

1. It was a good year for what type of flower in Elvis Costello's hit?

    a. Sunflowers   *b.* Roses   *c.* Tulips

2. Which of these girls names does *not* feature in the lyrics to The Beautiful South's 'Song For Whoever'?

    a. Jennifer   *b.* Julie   *c.* Barbara

3. Where exactly in the street did Madness live in 'Our House'?

    a. The corner   *b.* The end   *c.* The middle

4. When Stevie Wonder sang his only solo British No. 1 'I Just Called To Say I Love You', he meant it from the bottom of where?

    a. His heart   *b.* His soul   *c.* His mind

5. Which form of dance do Wham! sing about on their chart-topping 'Wake Me Up Before You Go-Go'?

    a. Funky Chicken   *b.* Boogaloo   *c.* Jitterbug

6. In Soul II Soul's 1989 hit 'Back To Life', where should you next go back to?

    a. Normality   *b.* Reality   *c.* Locality

7. According to Prince's 'Kiss', which US TV show is linked to having an attitude?

    a. Dallas   *b.* Falcon Crest   *c.* Dynasty

For answers see p299

8. **In The Proclaimers' 'Letter From America', where did the railtrack lead?**

    a. Miami to Canada

    b. Texas To Montreal

    c. Vegas to Buffalo

9. **Who would have blushed according to The Smiths' 'Heaven Knows I'm Miserable Now'?**

    a. Nero   *b.* Caesar   *c.* Caligula

10. **'Modern Love' gets David Bowie to where on time?**

    a. The shops   *b.* The church   *c.* The car

For answers see p299

1988

1. **Who starred in the film *Sign O' The Times*?**

   a. Madonna   *b.* Prince   *c.* Cher

2. **Perri McKissack was the real name of which hit-maker?**

   a. Mica Paris   *b.* Pebbles   *c.* Desireless

3. **Name Morrissey's first solo single.**

   a. 'Last Of The Famous International Playboys'

   b. 'Suedehead'   *c.* 'Everyday Is Like Sunday'

4. **Name the last Top 20 hit by Mel & Kim.**

   a. 'FLM'   *b.* 'Respectable'   *c.* 'That's The Way It Is'

5. **'Stop' hit-maker Sam Brown was the daughter of which '60s star?**

   a. Joe Brown   *b.* Marty Wilde   *c.* James Brown

6. **Nathan Moore led the group whose first Top 20 hit was 'The Harder I Try'. Name them.**

   a. The Christians   *b.* Prefab Sprout   *c.* Brother Beyond

7. **Which of these singers became the youngest US female to top the UK singles chart?**

   a. Debbie Gibson   *b.* Tiffany   *c.* Belinda Carlisle

For answers see p299

8. **Which famous record producer starred in the TV show *The Hitman And Her*?**

   a. Pete Waterman   b. Malcolm McLaren   c. Jonathan King

9. **Who hit the Top 20 with the charity record 'Running All Over The World'?**

   a. Wet Wet Wet   b. Tears For Fears   c. Status Quo

10. **Which famous '60s act was elected mayor of Palm Springs?**

   a. Roy Orbison   b. Sonny Bono   c. Gene Pitney

For answers see p299

1986 ALBUMS

1. **Name the singer who became the first UK female to amass nine chart albums in the '80s?**

   a. Kate Bush   *b.* Barbara Dickson   *c.* Elkie Brooks

2. **Name Bon Jovi's first Top 20 album.**

   a. Slippery When Wet   *b.* New Jersey   *c.* Keep The Faith

3. **Whose self-titled album spent 14 weeks at the top of the US chart this year?**

   a. Prince   *b.* Madonna   *c.* Whitney Houston

4. **With which act do you associate the album *Graceland*?**

   a. Elvis Presley   *b.* Grace Jones   *c.* Paul Simon

5. **'Papa Don't Preach' came from which Madonna album?**

   a. Like A Virgin   *b.* True Blue   *c.* Who's That Girl

6. ***Word Up* was Cameo's big album this year. Name their frontman.**

   a. Jeffrey Daniels   *b.* Larry Blackmon   *c.* Robert Bell

7. **Which top-selling album act was named Top British Group at the 1986 BRIT Awards?**

   a. U2   *b.* Dire Straits   *c.* Tears For Fears

8. **Michael Hutchence was voted Hunkiest Rock Singer. Which group did he sing with?**

   a. Europe   *b.* Supertramp   *c.* INXS

For answers see p300

9. Complete the title of Five Star's chart-topping album: *Silk And* _____.

   a. Satin   b. Steel   c. Milk

10. Whose chart-topping Greatest Hits album was called *Street Life*?

    a. Bryan Ferry & Roxy Music

    b. The Crusaders

    c. Randy Crawford

For answers see p300

MATCH THE GROUPS
AND THEIR TOP 10 HITS

1. Godley & Creme

2. Alphaville

3. The Blow Monkeys

4. Altered Images

5. The Cure

6. The Beat

7. Dollar

8. Bardo

9. Eighth Wonder

10. Bros

'Wedding Bells'   'Big In Japan'   'Too Much'

'O L'Amour'   'One Step Further'   'I'm Not Scared'

'Can't Get Used To Losing You'   'I Could Be Happy'

'The Love Cats'   'It Doesn't Have To Be This Way'

For answers see p300

 **TV & FILM**

1. Who sang about the unlikely TV superhero 'Super Gran'?

   a. Billy Connolly   *b.* Jasper Carrott   *c.* The Wurzels

2. Who had a 1987 top five hit with 'Crockett's Theme'?

   a. Clannad   *b.* Don Johnson   *c.* Jan Hammer

3. Who had a top ten hit with 'Arthur's Theme (Best That You Can Do)' in 1982, from the film of the same name?

   a. Chris Peacock   *b.* Kris Kristofferson   *c.* Christopher Cross

4. Mike Oldfield had a hit with the theme tune to which popular BBC children's show?

   a. Jackanory   *b.* Grange Hill   *c.* Blue Peter

5. Prince's 'Batdance' was taken from which film?

   a. Flashdance   *b.* Spider-Man   *c.* Batman

6. 'On Our Own' was the theme from *Ghostbusters II*. Who sang it?

   a. Whitney Houston   *b.* Bobby Brown   *c.* Michael Jackson

For answers see p300

7. **Who sang the theme to 1989 James Bond film *Licence To Kill*?**

   a. Tina Turner   *b.* Shirley Bassey   *c.* Gladys Knight

8. **The Four Tops' 'Loco In Acapulco' was taken from which British film?**

   a. Get Carter   *b.* Buster   *c.* The Long Good Friday

9. **Scott and Charlene were married in *Neighbours* to a song by Angry Anderson. Name it.**

   a. 'White Wedding'

   b. 'Here Comes The Bride'

   c. 'Suddenly'

10. **'Flashdance . . . What A Feeling' reached No. 2 in 1983 for which US singer?**

   a. Candi Staton   *b.* Irene Cara   *c.* Roberta Flack

For answers see p300

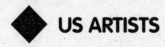 **US ARTISTS**

1. **What are Hall & Oates's christian names?**
   - *a.* Paul & Art
   - *b.* Daryl & John
   - *c.* Michael & Janet

2. **Stevie Nicks was a member of which group?**
   - *a.* Fleetwood Mac
   - *b.* Starship
   - *c.* Blondie

3. **Kim Carnes sang about whose eyes?**
   - *a.* Bette Midler
   - *b.* Audrey Hepburn
   - *c.* Bette Davis

4. **Who duetted with Prince on 'U Got The Look' in 1987?**
   - *a.* Sheena Easton
   - *b.* Martika
   - *c.* Susanna Hoffs

5. **Susanna Hoffs was the lead singer with which American group?**
   - *a.* The Go-Gos
   - *b.* The Bangles
   - *c.* Starship

6. **What repetitive-sounding group sang 'Broken Wings'?**
   - *a.* The The
   - *b.* Talk Talk
   - *c.* Mr Mister

For answers see p301

7. **Debbie Harry was the lead singer with which New York punk band?**

    a. The Bangles   b. The Go-Gos   c. Blondie

8. **What is Bruce Springsteen's middle name?**

    a. John   b. Michael   c. Joseph

9. **Lionel Richie was a member of which group before going solo?**

    a. The Commodores

    b. The Communards

    c. The Commitments

10. **Who showed her 'True Colors' in 1986?**

    a. Pat Benatar   b. Whitney Houston   c. Cyndi Lauper

For answers see p301

 **1989**

1. **Who co-hosted the shambolic BRIT Awards show with Samantha Fox?**

   a. Ben Elton   *b.* Mick Fleetwood   *c.* Jive Bunny

2. **Who had a hit with 'Waiting For A Star To Fall'?**

   a. Girl Meets Boy   *b.* The Boys & Girls   *c.* Boy Meets Girl

3. **Which act were credited with Bananarama on the charity hit 'Help'?**

   a. French & Saunders

   b. La Na Nee Nee Noo Noo

   c. Bombalurina

4. **'Eternal Flame' was a No. 1 for which group?**

   a. The Go-Gos   *b.* The Bangles   *c.* The Reynolds Girls

5. **Complete the name of the very successful production team: Stock, _____ & Waterman.**

   a. Lock   *b.* Aitken   *c.* Martin

For answers see p301

6. **Who was 'The Best' singer in 1989?**

   a. Bonnie Tyler   b. Tina Turner   c. Gladys Knight

7. **Mike & The Mechanics' vocalist Paul Carrack had previously sung on which Top 10 single?**

   a. 'In A Broken Dream' – Python Lee Jackson

   b. 'How Long' – Ace   c. 'Everything I Own' – Plastic Penny

8. **Which Scandinavian act gave us 'The Look' this year?**

   a. ABBA   b. Roxette   c. Europe

9. **Name the first hit by 808 State.**

   a. 'The Only Rhyme That Bites'   b. 'Cubik'   c. 'Pacific'

10. **What was special about Cliff Richard's 'The Best Of Me'?**

   a. It was the first hit he composed himself

   b. It was his 100th single

   c. It was his first single release to miss the Top 75

For answers see p301

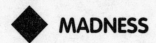 **MADNESS**

1. 'Night Boat To _____'

   a. Istanbul   b. Cairo   c. Casablanca

2. 'Baggy _____'

   a. Jumper   b. Vest   c. Trousers

3. 'The Return Of The Los Palmas _____'

   a. Seven   b. Five   c. Three

4. '_____ Day'

   a. Happy   b. Mad   c. Grey

5. 'Driving In My _____'

   a. Car   b. Limousine   c. 4x4

6. '_____ (Is All In The Mind)'

   a. Depression   b. Failure   c. Madness

7. 'Wings Of A _____'

   a. Butterfly   b. Dove   c. Fairy

8. 'I _____ You'

   a. Denounce   b. Renounce   c. Pronounce

9. '_____' (actor's name)

   a. Roger Moore   b. Spencer Tracy   c. Michael Caine

10. '_____ Girl'

    a. Tomorrow's   b. Sexy   c. Sweetest

For answers see p301

GIRL POWER
MATCH THE LADIES AND THEIR TOP 10 HITS

1. Kelly Marie

2. Laura Branigan

3. Kim Wilde

4. Laurie Anderson

5. Kate Robbins & Beyond

6. Kate Bush

7. Kylie Minogue

8. Lisa Stansfield

9. Kirsty MacColl

10. Madonna

'All Around The World'   'Dress You Up'

'Babooshka'   'Got To Be Certain'   'A New England'

'Gloria'   'Feels Like I'm In Love'   'Four Letter Word'

'O Superman'   'More Than In Love'

For answers see p302

NO. 1 SINGLES

1.   Who took 'Let's Party' to No. 1?

    a. David Bowie   *b.* Jive Bunny   *c.* Pat & Mick

2.   'Turtle Power' was taken to the top by which act?

    a. Partners In Business

    b. Partners In Kryme

    c. Partners In Law

3.   Which capital city had a 1986 chart-topping act named after it?

    a. London   *b.* Paris   *c.* Berlin

4.   Which of these Bucks Fizz tracks never reached No. 1?

    a. 'The Land Of Make Believe'

    b. 'Now Those Days Are Gone'

    c. 'Making Your Mind Up'

5.   In 1985, what was Paul Hardcastle's lucky number?

    a. '3'   *b.* '7'   *c.* '19'

For answers see p302

6. **What was the name of the singer who reached No. 1 with 'A Little Peace'?**

   a. Charlene   *b.* Robin Beck   *c.* Nicole

7. **What 21st-century TV show was named after a 1980 chart-topper by David Bowie?**

   a. Life On Mars   *b.* Ashes To Ashes   *c.* Fame

8. **What was the name of Rod Stewart's chart-topping baby in 1983?**

   a. 'Maggie May'   *b.* 'Ruby Tuesday'   *c.* 'Baby Jane'

9. **The Emerald Express were given an artist credit on whose No. 1 single?**

   a. Enya   *b.* Dexy's Midnight Runners   *c.* Johnny Logan

10. **The Bee Gees only had one chart-topper in the '80s. Name it.**

   a. 'Tragedy'   *b.* 'Night Fever'   *c.* 'You Win Again'

For answers see p302

 **DANCE**

1. **Complete the name of this 1986 dance music hit-maker: Farley '_____' Funk.**

   a. Housemaster   *b.* Mastermixer   *c.* Jackmaster

2. **In 1983, Forrest charted with 'Rock The Boat'. Who had the original 1974 version?**

   a. George McCrae

   b. The Hues Corporation

   c. The Gap Band

3. **Who was 'Dancing Tight' in 1983?**

   a. Kool & The Gang   *b.* Mary Jane Girls

   c. Phil Fearon & Galaxy

4. **Name the big hit associated with Man 2 Man meet Man Parrish?**

   a. 'Male Stripper'   *b.* 'Walk The Dinosaur'   *c.* 'Crush On You'

5. **Who wanted to 'Shake You Down' in 1986?**

   a. Grandmaster Flash

   b. Gregory Abbott

   c. Colonel Abrams

For answers see p302

6. On Jellybean's 1987 hit, 'Who Found Who', who joined him on vocals?

    a. Steven Dante   *b.* Elisa Fiorillo   *c.* Adele Bertei

7. What was the name of the act that had a Top 5 hit with 'House Arrest' in 1987?

    a. Krush   *b.* Stock, Aitken & Waterman   *c.* M/A/R/R/S

8. Complete the title of Lil Louis 1989 dance hit: '_____ Kiss'.

    a. French   *b.* Your   *c.* Kiss

9. Which act had a chart-topping 1989 album with *Club Classics Vol. 1*?

    a. Soul II Soul   *b.* Kool & The Gang   *c.* Cameo

10. Who was 'Into The Groove' in 1985?

    a. Loose Ends   *b.* Midnight Star   *c.* Madonna

For answers see p302

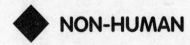 **NON-HUMAN**

1. **Which of these is a correct instruction from the chorus of Spitting Image's 'The Chicken Song'?**

   a. Stick a sofa up your nose   *b.* Casserole your gran

   c. Pretend your name is Alan

2. **What was the title of the debut release by the rabbit-attired Jive Bunny & The Mastermixers?**

   a. 'That Sounds Good To Me'

   b. 'Swing The Mood'

   c. 'That's What I Like'

3. **The Housemartins' chart bow in 1986 was the name of which animal?**

   a. Horse   *b.* Cow   *c.* Sheep

4. **Name Chas & Dave's first Top 10 single.**

   a. 'Rabbit'   *b.* 'Fox'   *c.* 'Hare'

5. **What colour was Orville the duck, who partnered Keith Harris on the 1982 hit 'Orville's Song'?**

   a. Purple   *b.* Orange   *c.* Green

For answers see p303

6. **UB40 had their hands full with a rat in 1987, but in which room was the rodent found?**

   a. Bathroom   b. Kitchen   c. Bedroom

7. **'Hokey Cokey' was memorably performed on *Top Of The Pops* in 1981 by a group of what?**

   a. Snowmen   b. Wombles   c. Aliens

8. **By what name is Marillion vocalist Derek Dick better known?**

   a. The Cat   b. Fish   c. Linx

9. **Paul McCartney 'stood together' with a chorus of which sort of amphibians in 1984?**

   a. Toads   b. Newts   c. Frogs

10. **Name the feathered vocalists who introduced us to 'The Birdie Song (The Birdie Dance)'.**

    a. The Birdies   b. The Birds   c. The Tweets

For answers see p303

 **DANCE**

1. **What was the name of Lipps Inc's No. 2 hit in 1980?**

   a. 'Boogie Oogie Oogie'   *b.* 'Funky Town'

   c. 'Never Knew Love Like This Before'

2. **'We Call It Acieed' was a hit for which mob?**

   a. E Mob   *b.* G Mob   *c.* D Mob

3. **Which of the following was the title of a Break Machine hit?**

   a. 'Street Dance'   *b.* 'Break Dance'

   c. 'Breakin' . . . There's No Stopping Us'

4. **Who made their 'Body Talk' in 1981?**

   a. Imagination   *b.* Evelyn King   *c.* Yarbrough & Peoples

5. **Who had a disco hit in 1982 with 'Can't Take My Eyes Off You'?**

   a. Frankie Valli   *b.* Boys Town Gang   *c.* Gloria Gaynor

For answers see p303

6. 'Let The Music Play' was a big club hit in 1983 for whom?

a. The Rocksteady Crew   b. Shannon   c. Forrest

7. Where is the 'Electric Avenue' that Eddy Grant sang about?

a. Kingston, Jamaica   b. Harlem   c. Brixton

8. Who was 'Trapped' on their only Top 20 hit?

a. Cameo   b. Colonel Abrams   c. Steve Arrington

9. What is the correct title of the biggest hit by Rocker's Revenge?

a. 'Walking On Sunshine'

b. 'Walking On The Moon'

c. 'Walk On The Milky Way'

10. Who taught us how to do the 'Lambada'?

a. Kaoma   b. Kon Kan   c. Fresh 4

For answers see p303

 **1980**

1. **Name the Stray Cats' first hit.**

    a. 'Rock This Town'   *b.* 'Runaway Boys'   *c.* 'Stray Cat Strut'

2. **Before her solo hits, Randy Crawford was vocalist with which jazz act on the hit 'Street Life'?**

    a. Herbie Hancock   *b.* Roy Ayres   *c.* The Crusaders

3. **Hazel O'Connor had three Top 20 hits. Name the first one.**

    a. 'D-Days'   *b.* 'Eighth Day'   *c.* 'Will You?'

4. **Who made his Top 20 debut with 'Give Me The Night'?**

    a. Jermaine Jackson   *b.* George Benson

    c. Narada Michael Walden

5. **What TV show was Dennis Waterman's hit 'I Could Be So Good For You' featured in?**

    a. The Sweeney   *b.* Minder   *c.* New Tricks

For answers see p303

6. Who took the Ronettes song 'Be My Baby' back into the Top 10?

a. Stiff Little Fingers   b. The Ramones   c. The Nolans

7. Name the last Top 20 hit by Dr Hook.

a. 'Sexy Eyes'

b. 'When You're In Love With A Beautiful Woman'

c. 'Better Love Next Time'

8. Name the Yellow Magic Orchestra's only Top 20 hit.

a. 'Computer Game'   b. 'Jazz Carnival'

c. 'Check Out The Groove'

9. Name the group who took us to the 'D.I.S.C.O.'.

a. Ottaman   b. Ottawan   c. Ottavan

10. Which US R&B act made everyone 'Stomp'?

a. The Gap Band   b. Positive Force   c. Brothers Johnson

For answers see p303

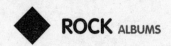 **ROCK** ALBUMS

1. *American Fool,* containing the song 'Hurts So Good', was a hit album for whom?

    a. John Cougar   *b.* David Lee Roth   *c.* Dennis DeYoung

2. Which group gave us *The Number Of The Beast*?

    a. AC/DC   *b.* Iron Maiden   *c.* Black Sabbath

3. *Live Evil* was an album from Ozzy Osbourne's colourful band. Name them.

    a. Whitesnake   *b.* Black Sabbath   *c.* Deep Purple

4. Bryan Ferry's group released *Avalon* this year. Name them.

    a. Poxy Music   *b.* Roxy Music   *c.* Toxic Music

5. Who won a Grammy for their *IV* album?

    a. Boston   *b.* Journey   *c.* Toto

6. Who released *Mirage* but couldn't repeat the success of *Rumours* and *Tusk*?

    a. Huey Lewis & The News

    b. Fleetwood Mac

    c. Van Halen

For answers see p304

7. What material were Billy Joel's curtains made from?

   a. Cotton   *b.* Nylon   *c.* Wool

8. The Jam in 1982 and Midge Ure in 1985 shared which album title?

   a. Malice   *b.* Vienna   *c.* The Gift

9. Which one-time Yes member won a BRIT award for Best British Producer?

   a. Trevor Horn   *b.* Trevor Corn   *c.* Trevor Born

10. Aerosmith were on a what in 1987?

    a. Extended Period Of Leave   *b.* Short Break

    c. Permanent Vacation

For answers see p304

COMPLETE THE TITLE SINGLES

1. 'We Don't Need Another _____' (Tina Turner)

      a. Drink   *b.* Hero   *c.* Quiz Book

2. 'Dancing In The_____' (David Bowie & Mick Jagger)

      a. Club   *b.* Street   *c.* Night

3. '_____ In The Sky' (Doctor & The Medics)

      a. Lucy   *b.* High   *c.* Spirit

4. 'The Lady In _____' (Chris de Burgh)

      a. Bed   *b.* Love   *c.* Red

5. 'Under The _____' Bruce Willis

      a. Stars   *b.* Boardwalk   *c.* Bed

6. 'Pump Up The _____' (M/A/R/R/S)

      a. Bitter   *b.* Tyres   *c.* Volume

7. 'Don't Turn _____' (Aswad)

      a. Away   *b.* Around   *c.* Japanese

8. 'Beat _____' (Bomb The Bass)

      a. It   *b.* Dis   *c.* Dat

9. '_____ And Wine' (Cliff Richard)

      a. Cheese   *b.* Mistletoe   *c.* Beer

10. 'Only _____' (Nana Mouskouri)

      a. Love   *b.* You   *c.* One

For answers see 304

FILL IN THE GAPS
FAMOUS PEOPLE / NAMES

1. 'I Feel Like _____' (Alvin Stardust)

2. '_____ Boy' (Baltimora)

3. '_____'s Waiting' (Bananarama)

4. '_____' (Madness)

5. 'Wood Beez (Pray Like _____)' (Scritti Politti)

6. '_____' (Michael Jackson)

7. '_____ (Is A Weatherman)' (Tribe of Toffs)

8. '_____' (Nik Kershaw)

9. '_____' Special AKA

10. 'I Wanna Be A _____' (Screaming Blue Messiahs)

Michael Caine   Nelson Mandela

Aretha Franklin   Billie Jean   Buddy Holly

Don Quixote   John Kettley   Flintstone

Robert De Niro   Tarzan

For answers see p304

STATUS QUO

1. _____ **Gold Bars** (album)

   a. 3   b. 12   c. 50

2. 'What You're _____ '

   a. Suggesting   b. Proposing   c. Saying

3. 'Lies ' / 'Don't _____'

   a. Waste My Time   b. Drive My Car   c. Pick This One

4. 'Dear _____'

   a. John   b. Jack   c. James

5. 'The _____'

   a. Rule-Breaker   b. Wild One   c. Wanderer

6. '_____ Sky'

   a. Night   b. Red   c. Cloudy

7. '_____ All Over The World' (1988)

   a. Rockin'   b. Running   c. Strumming

8. 'Ol' Rag _____'

   a. Blues   b. Time   c. Song

9. 'A Mess Of _____'

   a. Dreams   b. Rock   c. Blues

10. 'Who Gets _____?'

    a. The Boogie   b. The Love   c. The Vibe

For answers see p305

1987 ALBUMS

1. Who had the first of several Top 10 albums with *Popped In Souled Out*?

   a. Erasure   *b.* Beastie Boys   *c.* Wet Wet Wet

2. Identify the word missing from this Fleetwood Mac album: _____ *In The Night*.

   a. Strangers   *b.* Dancing   *c.* Tango

3. Who made *Music For The Masses*?

   a. Lloyd Cole & The Commotions

   b. Depeche Mode

   c. The Pretenders

4. Which of these 1987 albums spent the most time at No. 1 in the US?

   a. Dirty Dancing (soundtrack)

   b. Whitney – Whitney Houston

   c. Bad – Michael Jackson

5. What was named Best British Album at the 1987 BRIT Awards?

   a. So – Peter Gabriel   *b.* Picture Book – Simply Red

   c. Brothers In Arms – Dire Straits

6. *Better To Travel* was a No. 1 album for which act?

   a. The Christians   *b.* New Order   *c.* Swing Out Sister

For answers see p305

7. **U2's long-awaited album sold 250,000 in the first week. Name it.**

   a. Rattle And Hum

   b. The Unforgettable Fire

   c. The Joshua Tree

8. **Which US R&B singer had a Top 10 album called *Hearsay*?**

   a. Luther Vandross   b. Alexander O'Neal   c. Lionel Richie

9. ***One To One* was the last of three Top 10 albums for which act?**

   a. Howard Jones   b. Sigue Sigue Sputnik   c. Shalamar

10. **Complete the title of this No. 1 Simple Minds album: *Live In The* _____.**

    a. Park   b. City Of Light   c. Studio

For answers see p305

1981

1. **Phil Collins had his first solo hit this year. Name it.**

   a. 'You Can't Hurry Love'

   b. 'In The Air Tonight'

   c. 'I Missed Again'

2. **Which show did Elaine Paige's hit 'Memory' come from?**

   a. Starlight Express   b. Cats   c. Phantom Of The Opera

3. **Complete this Gary Numan hit title: 'She's Got _____'.**

   a. Everything   b. Claws   c. You

4. **Who introduced us to the 'Kids In America'?**

   a. Blondie   b. Toyah   c. Kim Wilde

5. **The classic Dion song 'Runaround Sue' was the last hit for which '70s 'teenybop' band?**

   a. The Sweet   b. Mud   c. Racey

6. **Complete this sentence: In the US, The Human League's 'Don't You Want Me' _____**

   a. Was a flop   b. Was banned   c. Was a No. 1

7. **'I'm Coming Out' was whose assertion in 1981?**

   a. Debby Boone   b. Kiki Dee   c. Diana Ross

8. **What did the title of Haircut 100's hit 'Favourite Shirts' have in brackets?**

   a. (When I Go Out)   b. (That I Wear)   c. (Boy Meets Girl)

For answers see p305

9. Which of these Matchbox hits was the last to reach the Top 20?

a. 'When You Ask About Love'   *b.* 'Rockabilly Rebel'

c. 'Over The Rainbow – You Belong To Me'

10. Which singer/songwriter wrote and originally recorded Kim Carnes's hit 'Bette Davis Eyes'?

a. Carole King   *b.* Jackie DeShannon   *c.* Melanie

For answers see p305

NOVELTY/ONE-HIT WONDERS

1. **Which TV comedian scored with 'Loadsamoney'?**

    a. Ben Elton   *b.* Harry Enfield   *c.* Paul Whitehouse

2. **Who was the act whose one hit was called 'Tarzan Boy'?**

    a. Fiddler's Dram   *b.* Baltimora   *c.* Nu Shooz

3. **Whose one hit was 'Et Les Oiseaux Chantaient (And The Birds Were Singing)'?**

    a. The Tweets   *b.* The Sweet People

    c. St Winifred's School Choir

4. **Which act had a Top 10 hit with the novelty record 'Do The Conga'?**

    a. Bad Manners   *b.* Black Lace

    c. Jive Bunny & The Mastermixers

5. **Which of these was *not* the title of a Starsound hit?**

    a. 'Stars on 45'   *b.* 'Stars On Stevie'

    c. 'Stars On The Beatles'

6. **Which European superstar had their only UK Top 20 single in 1986 with 'Only Love'?**

    a. Sacha Distel   *b.* Julio Iglesias   *c.* Nana Mouskouri

7. **Complete the name of the one-hit wonder who released 'Baby I Love Your Way'/'Freebird': Will To _____.**

    a. Won't   *b.* Succeed   *c.* Power

For answers see p306

8. **Who did David Bowie team up with for the hit 'Peace On Earth'/'Little Drummer Boy'?**

   a. Mick Jagger   *b.* Queen   *c.* Bing Crosby

9. **The singer of the 1987 hit 'Call Me' was Ivana Spagna. What was her recording name?**

   a. Ivana   *b.* Spagna   *c.* Mirage

10. **Which of these one-hit wonders was *not* French?**

    a. Denise LaSalle   *b.* F.R. David   *c.* Ryan Paris

For answers see p306

1982

1. **What was the sub-title of David Bowie's 'Cat People'?**

   a. Putting Out Whiskas   *b.* Putting Out Fire

   c. Putting Out Kittens

2. **Who won this year's Eurovision Song Contest?**

   a. Bucks Fizz   *b.* The Herries   *c.* Nicole

3. **Complete the name of the following group: Joan Jett & The _____.**

   a. Rockets   *b.* Jetsons   *c.* Blackhearts

4. **Who wrote a 'Classic' in 1982?**

   a. Boy George   *b.* Gary Numan   *c.* Adrian Gurvitz

5. **Who collaborated with Fun Boy Three on 'Really Saying Something'?**

   a. Haircut 100   *b.* Bananarama   *c.* Heaven 17

6. **Who lied by saying 'This Time (We'll Get It Right)', but didn't?**

   a. Bucks Fizz

   b. England World Cup Squad

   c. The Human League

7. **Valerie Landsberg was the credited vocalist for which hit act?**

   a. Bardo   *b.* Toto Coelo   *c.* The Kids From Fame

For answers see p306

8. **Who composed Dionne Warwick's big hit 'Heartbreaker'?**

   a. Gamble & Huff

   b. Bacharach & David

   c. The Gibb Brothers

9. **What did Simple Minds promise us this year?**

   a. An Album   *b.* A Single   *c.* A Miracle

10. **Which national football team sang 'We Have A Dream'?**

    a. Scotland   *b.* Northern Ireland   *c.* England

For answers see p306

PET SHOP BOYS

1. 'West End _____'

    a. Girls   *b.* Boys   *c.* Chippy

2. '_____ Comes Quickly'

    a. Death   *b.* Love   *c.* Neil

3. 'Opportunities (Let's Make Lots Of _____)'

    a. Noise   *b.* Cash   *c.* Money

4. 'What Have I Done To Deserve _____?'

    a. Your Love   *b.* This   *c.* Your Devotion

5. '_____ On My Mind'

    a. Forever   *b.* Always   *c.* Gentle

6. '_____ Dancing'

    a. Domino   *b.* Tiddlywink   *c.* Marble

7. 'Left To My Own _____'

    a. Thoughts   *b.* Choices   *c.* Devices

8. 'It's _____'

    a. Alright   *b.* Terrible   *c.* Driving Me Slightly Mad

9. 'Two _____ Zero'

    a. Divided by   *b.* One   *c.* Times

10. '_____' (London tube station)

    a. Camden Town   *b.* Angel   *c.* King's Cross

For answers see p306

FILL IN THE GAPS
COLOURS

1. '99 _____ Balloons' (Nena)

2. 'Fade To _____' (Visage)

3. '_____ Door' (Shakin' Stevens)

4. 'Hi-De-Hi (Holiday Rock)' (Paul Shane & The _____coats)

5. '_____ Eyes' (Elton John)

6. '_____ Wedding' (Billy Idol)

7. 'Rip It Up' (_____ Juice)

8. '_____ Rain' (Prince & The Revolution)

9. 'Wonderful Life' (_____)

10. 'Pretty In _____' (The Psychedelic Furs)

Blue   Green   Red   White

Black   Pink   Purple   Orange

Yellow   Grey

For answers see p307

1983

1. **What was The Smiths' first release?**

   a. 'Hand In Glove'   *b.* 'This Charming Man'

   c. 'What Difference Does It Make'

2. **Who had the first of eight Top 20 entries with 'Fields Of Fire'?**

   a. Culture Club   *b.* Heaven 17   *c.* Big Country

3. **The title of the Level 42 hit 'The Sun Goes Down' is completed by which bracketed words?**

   a. (The Moon Comes Up)   *b.* (Living It Up)   *c.* (We Stay Up)

4. **The UK's Eurovision entry for this year, 'Never Giving Up', was performed by which act?**

   a. Bardo   *b.* Sweet Dreams   *c.* Belle & The Devotions

5. **Who sang on Mike Oldfield's hit 'Moonlight Shadow'?**

   a. Anita Hegerland   *b.* Maggie Reilly   *c.* Sally Oldfield

6. **Whose last Top 20 entry was called 'Our Lips Are Sealed'?**

   a. The Bangles   *b.* Fun Boy Three   *c.* Bananarama

7. **Pete Burns fronted which much-talked about band?**

   a. Dead Or Alive   *b.* Blancmange

   c. Echo & The Bunnymen

8. **What was Kajagoogoo's follow-up to 'Too Shy'?**

   a. 'Ooh To Be Ah'   *b.* 'Hang On Now'   *c.* 'Big Apple'

For answers see p307

9. **What was the name of Malcolm McLaren's backing group?**

a. McLaren Team   *b.* Malc's Mob

c. The World's Famous Supreme Team

10. **Who had their only Top 20 hit with 'Calling Your Name'?**

a. Tracie   *b.* Marilyn   *c.* F. R. David

For answers see p307

ROCK ALBUMS

1. **Deep Purple scored their third Top 10 album of the '80s with which title?**

   a. The House Of Blue Light   b. Steel Wheels

   c. The Unforgettable Fire

2. **Gillan were on the *Glory Road* in 1980, but what was the first name of the vocalist whose surname christened the band?**

   a. Ozzy   b. Ian   c. Bill

3. **Who released the albums *Flush The Fashion, Special Forces, Dada, Constrictor* and *Raise Your Fist And Yell*?**

   a. David Coverdale   b. Bruce Dickinson   c. Alice Cooper

4. **Delilah was nowhere to be found, but which band, who released *Head On* in 1980, was named after their vocalist and guitarist?**

   a. Samson   b. Tommy Scott & The Senators

   c. The Sensational Alex Harvey Band

5. **What was the one-word title of INXS's first Top 10 album, released in 1987?**

   a. Disappear   b. Kick   c. Mystify

6. **The late Jimi Hendrix returned to the Top 20 in 1982 with which live album?**

   a. The Jimi Hendrix Concerts   b. Blues   c. BBC Sessions

For answers see p307

7. In the Dire Straits hit 'Money For Nothing' from their album *Brothers In Arms*, what was free?

   a. Chips   *b.* Cheques   *c.* Chicks

8. Which band, who were once 'On The Threshold Of A Dream', released the album *Long Distance Voyager* in 1981?

   a. The Moody Blues   *b.* Roxy Music

   c. Electric Light Orchestra

9. Def Leppard, the group who created *Hysteria*, hailed from which UK city?

   a. Liverpool   *b.* Hull   *c.* Sheffield

10. Identify the colour that's the title of a 1988 album by R.E.M.

   a. Orange   *b.* Green   *c.* Purple

For answers see p307

FILL IN THE GAPS

NUMBERS (ALBUMS)

1. _____ And The Ragged Tiger (Duran Duran)

2. The Luxury Gap (Heaven _____)

3. Cupid And Psyche _____ (Scritti Politti)

4. London 0 Hull _____ (The Housemartins)

5. _____ Feet High And Rising (De La Soul)

6. The _____ Legged Groove Machine (The Wonder Stuff)

7. Pelican West (Haircut _____)

8. Stars On _____ (Starsound)

9. Blind Man's Zoo (_____ Maniacs)

10. _____ (Depeche Mode)

3	4	7	8
17	45	85	100
	101	10,000	

For answers see p308

1988 ALBUMS

1. **Fish left which act this year?**

    a. Big Country   *b.* Marillion   *c.* The Mission

2. **Finish the name of this 1987 chart-topping act: Johnny Hates _____.**

    a. Pop quiz books   *b.* Chelsea   *c.* Jazz

3. **Who had a hit album called *Now That's What I Call Quite Good!*?**

    a. Morrissey   *b.* The Housemartins   *c.* Pet Shop Boys

4. **Complete this sentence: In the US, George Michael's *Faith* album _____.**

    a. Failed to chart

    b. Was No. 1 for 12 weeks

    c. Sold less than 50,000

5. **Who 'introduced' us to 'the hardline'?**

    a. Terence Trent D'Arby   *b.* Metallica   *c.* Public Enemy

For answers see p308

6. **What did AC/DC suggest we blow up?**

    a. Your House   *b.* Your CD Player   *c.* Your Video

7. **Whose last Top 10 album was called *Roll With It*?**

    a. Steve Winwood   *b.* Joy Division   *c.* The Bangles

8. **Axl Rose fronted which successful band?**

    a. Rose Tattoo   *b.* Rose Royce   *c.* Guns N' Roses

9. **Complete this Dire Straits album title: *Money For* _____.**

    a. Old Rope   *b.* Us   *c.* Nothing

10. **The BRIT Album of the Year award in 1988 went to which record?**

    a. *Faith* – George Michael

    b. *Actually* – Pet Shop Boys

    c. *Nothing Like The Sun* – Sting

For answers see p308

 **1984**

1. **Paul Weller organised a group who recorded 'Soul Deep' to help striking miners. Name the group.**

   a. Mine Aid   *b.* Council Collective   *c.* Weller's Helpers

2. **Name Alison Moyet's debut solo hit.**

   a. 'Love Resurrection'   *b.* 'All Cried Out'

   c. 'That Ole Devil Called Love'

3. **With whom did Michael Jackson share the vocals on the song 'State Of Shock' in 1984?**

   a. Stevie Wonder   *b.* Paul McCartney   *c.* Mick Jagger

4. **Who had a Top 5 hit in 1984 with 'Self Control'?**

   a. Jennifer Rush   *b.* Laura Branigan   *c.* Pat Benatar

5. **Complete this Shakatak title: 'Down On The _____'.**

   a. Beach Tonight   *b.* Farm   *c.* Street

For answers see p308

6. Who took a record seven Grammy Awards this year?

a. Quincy Jones   b. Michael Jackson   c. Bruce Springsteen

7. Who was 'Big In Japan'?

a. The Vapours   b. Alphaville   c. Fiction Factory

8. Which member of The Stray Cats married actress Britt Ekland?

a. Brian Setzer   b. Lee Rocker   c. Slim Jim Phantom

9. What was the last The Specials/The Special AKA single to reach the Top 20?

a. 'Nelson Mandela'   b. 'Ghost Town'   c. 'Do Nothing'

10. Janet Jackson released 'Two To The Power Of Love' with which already famous singer?

a. Cliff Richard   b. Michael Jackson   c. Marvin Gaye

For answers see p308

MATCH THE GROUPS AND THEIR TOP 10 HITS

1. Genesis

2. Associates

3. Climie Fisher

4. Bee Gees

5. a-ha

6. Club Nouveau

7. The Gap Band

8. Aztec Camera

9. Big Country

10. ABBA

'Big Fun'   'Cry Wolf'   'Lean On Me'   'Chance'

'Party Fears Two'   'You Win Again'   'Rise To The Occasion'

'One Of Us'   'Somewhere In My Heart'   'Mama'

For answers see p309

MATCH THE TOP 10 GROUP AND THEIR SINGER

1. Galaxy

2. PIL

3. Wet Wet Wet

4. The Police

5. Scritti Politti

6. Roxy Music

7. REO Speedwagon

8. Whitesnake

9. Sigue Sigue Sputnik

10. Simply Red

Martin Degville   David Coverdale   Mick Hucknall

Marti Pellow   Sting   Kevin Cronin   Bryan Ferry

Johnny Rotten   Phil Fearon   Green Gartside

For answers see p309

1985

1. **Which of these groups was a Duran Duran spin-off?**

   a. Red Box   *b.* Arcadia   *c.* Trans-X

2. **Which Marti Webb hit had previously charted for Michael Jackson?**

   a. 'One Day In Your Life'   *b.* 'Ben'   *c.* 'Always There'

3. **Britain's Eurovision Song Contest entry for this year was 'Love Is'. Who sang it?**

   a. Belle & The Devotions   *b.* Vikki   *c.* Ryder

4. **Who picked up the BRIT award for Best British Group?**

   a. Wham!   *b.* Frankie Goes To Hollywood   *c.* Black Lace

5. **Name Whitney Houston's first Top 20 entry.**

   a. 'I Wanna Dance With Somebody'   *b.* 'How Will I Know'

   c. 'Saving All My Love For You'

6. **Complete the sentence: In the US, 'Frankie' by Sister Sledge _____ .**

   a. Gave them their biggest hit

   b. Earned them a gold disc

   c. Did not reach the Top 40

For answers see p309

7. **Which of these acts did *not* appear at Live Aid?**

a. U2   b. Bruce Springsteen   c. Madonna

8. **Who originally recorded UB40's hit 'I Got You Babe'?**

a. Frank & Nancy Sinatra

b. Sonny & Cher

c. Esther & Abi Ofarim

9. **Elton John presented the Ivor Novello Songwriter of the Year award to which composer?**

a. Phil Collins   b. George Michael   c. Paul McCartney

10. **Complete the title of this Talking Heads hit: 'Road To _____'.**

a. London   b. Nowhere   c. Redemption

For answers see p309

GUESS THE ARTIST

1. Who was *Saved* before surviving a *Shot Of Love* in the early '80s?

   a. George Harrison   b. Elton John   c. Bob Dylan

2. Who was *Five Miles Out* and two places away from a Top 5 album in 1982?

   a. Mike Oldfield   b. Vangelis   c. Jean-Michel Jarre

3. Ray Burns and Dave Vanian were two members of which group?

   a. The Damned   b. The Fall   c. The Blockheads

4. Who encountered *Crocodiles*, a *Porcupine* and dancing horses in their '80s chart career?

   a. Echo & The Bunnymen

   b. The Tubeway Army

   c. Scritti Politti

5. Trevor Horn masterminded the '80s comeback of which 'lonely hearts' band?

   a. Yes   b. No   c. Maybe

For answers see p310

6. **Who released albums with Crazy Horse, The Shocking Pinks and The Blue Notes?**

   a. Bruce Springsteen   *b.* Neil Young   *c.* Elvis Costello

7. **Name the 'heat-seeking' group who famously missed the Top 10 with each of their 28 charting singles?**

   a. Killing Joke   *b.* AC/DC   *c.* New Model Army

8. **Who gave us 'The Message' in 1982?**

   a. Grandmaster Flash   *b.* Beastie Boys   *c.* Duran Duran

9. **Who were surveying the 'Manhattan Skyline'?**

   a. Brother Beyond   *b.* a-ha   *c.* A Flock Of Seagulls

10. **This stylish mod left his band in 1982 and then found himself in *Café Bleu* with Mick Talbot. Who is he?**

   a. Boy George   *b.* Morrissey   *c.* Paul Weller

For answers see p310

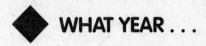 **WHAT YEAR . . .**

1.　. . .was Aled Jones 'Walking In The Air'?

　　　　　　　　　　a. 1983　　*b.* 1985　　*c.* 1987

2.　. . .did Band Aid II reach No. 1 with 'Do They Know It's Christmas'?

　　　　　　　　　　a. 1984　　*b.* 1985　　*c.* 1989

3.　. . .did Ben E. King top the chart with 'Stand By Me'?

　　　　　　　　　　a. 1982　　*b.* 1985　　*c.* 1987

4.　. . .did Bette Midler chart with 'Wind Beneath My Wings'?

　　　　　　　　　　a. 1984　　*b.* 1987　　*c.* 1989

5.　. . .was the Black Lace classic 'Agadoo'?

　　　　　　　　　　a. 1981　　*b.* 1984　　*c.* 1986

For answers see p310

6. . . .did Bob Marley's 'No Woman No Cry' reach the Top 10?

   a. 1986   b. 1981   c. 1983

7. . . .did Chris De Burgh score with 'The Lady In Red'?

   a. 1984   b. 1986   c. 1988

8. . . .did Cyndi Lauper tell us 'Girls Just Want To Have Fun'?

   a. 1984   b. 1989   c. 1986

9. . . .did Elaine Paige provide us with a 'Memory'?

   a. 1983   b. 1981   c. 1985

10. . . .did The Firm go 'Star Trekkin''?

   a. 1985   b. 1987   c. 1989

For answers see p310

NO. 1 SINGLES

1. **Ben E. King's 1987 No. 1 'Stand By Me' was first released in what year?**

   a. 1961 *b.* 1964 *c.* 1969

2. **What is Bonnie Tyler's real name?**

   a. Gwen Tyler *b.* Gaynor Hopkins *c.* Bonita Evans

3. **Complete the name of this chart-topping act: Fairground _____?**

   a. Ride *b.* Workers *c.* Attraction

4. **Who featured with Marc Almond on the No. 1 hit 'Something's Gotten Hold Of My Heart'?**

   a. Roy Orbison *b.* Soft Cell *c.* Gene Pitney

5. **What was the surname of chart-topping twins Mel & Kim?**

   a. Wilde *b.* Smith *c.* Appleby

For answers see p310

6. **Name the artist who took 'I Want To Wake Up With You' to the top?**

   a. Eddy Grant   *b.* Boris Gardiner   *c.* Desmond Dekker

7. **Which group hit the top with 'The Final Countdown'?**

   a. Asia   *b.* Europe   *c.* America

8. **What was the first track on *The Special AKA Live!* EP by The Specials?**

   a. 'Guns Of Navarone'

   b. 'Skinhead Moonstomp'

   c. 'Too Much Too Young'

9. **Name the record that brought fame to Irene Cara.**

   a. 'Ring My Bell'   *b.* 'Together We Are Beautiful'   *c.* 'Fame'

10. **Who wrote Barbra Streisand's No. 1 hit 'Woman In Love'?**

   a. Bacharach & David

   b. Lennon & McCartney

   c. Barry & Robin Gibb

For answers see p310

 **TV & FILM**

1. Which of the following artists never recorded a James Bond film theme during the '80s?

    a. Gladys Knight   *b.* Natalie Cole   *c.* Sheena Easton

2. Eighties hit-maker Hazel O'Connor launched her career in a rock music movie called *Breaking* _____.

    a. Glass   *b.* Wood   *c.* Steel

3. Al _____ sang the hit theme tune to the US detective TV series *Moonlighting*.

    a. Jarreau   *b.* Gore   *c.* Jolson

4. Berlin's 'Take My Breath Away' featured in the 1986 motion picture *Top* _____.

    a. Cat   *b.* Gun   *c.* Man

5. In 1986, which TV sitcom star reached No. 2 in the UK chart with 'Starting Together', the theme to a BBC TV documentary called *The Marriage*?

    a. Harry Enfield   *b.* Kathy Staff   *c.* Su Pollard

6. Who starred in, and wrote the screenplay for, a critically panned 1984 film called *Give My Regards To Broad Street*?

    a. Paul Weller   *b.* Paul McCartney   *c.* Paul Simon

For answers see p311

7. Which of these oldies did *not* get revived in a series of Levi Jeans TV adverts in the '80s?

a. 'I Heard It Through The Grapevine'

b. 'Wonderful World'

c. 'Donald Where's Your Troosers'

8. Robin Beck's chart-topper from 1988, 'The First Time', started life as a TV commercial advertising what?

a. Coca-Cola   b. Mobile phones   c. Toothpaste

9. Which of these Alison Moyet singles was originally the title theme from a 1945 film starring Joseph Cotten and Jennifer Jones?

a. 'Weak In The Presence Of Beauty'

b. 'Love Resurrection'   c. 'Love Letters'

10. Which group's only two UK hits, 'Eye Of The Tiger' and 'Burning Heart', both featured in Sylvester Stallone's series of *Rocky* films?

a. Survivor   b. J Geils Band   c. Journey

For answers see p311

COVER VERSIONS

1. **Boy George had a 1987 hit with his cover of 'Everything I Own'. Who took the song to number one in 1974?**

    a. David Gates   *b.* Ken Boothe   *c.* Paul Da Vinci

2. **According to Tight Fit's 1982 No. 1 cover hit, which animal sleeps tonight?**

    a. Tiger   *b.* Leopard   *c.* Lion

3. **Who wrote and originally recorded UB40's 1983 No. 1 hit 'Red Red Wine'?**

    a. Bernie Taupin   *b.* Diane Warren   *c.* Neil Diamond

4. **Who had a Top 5 hit in 1986 with 'Eloise'?**

    a. Barry Ryan   *b.* Peter Gabriel   *c.* The Damned

5. **Which band, whose name means 'The Wolves', had a No. 1 hit in 1987 with 'La Bamba'?**

    a. Baccara   *b.* Inti Illimani-Guamary   *c.* Los Lobos

For answers see p311

6. **Who originally recorded the Art Of Noise/Tom Jones 1988 hit 'Kiss'?**

   a. Sting   *b.* Prince   *c.* Erasure

7. **Who had the first hit with 'I Don't Want To Talk About It', the Everything But The Girl hit from 1988?**

   a. Tom Jones   *b.* Status Quo   *c.* Rod Stewart

8. **Blondie's 'The Tide Is High' was first recorded by whom?**

   a. The Paragons   *b.* The Pioneers   *c.* Prince Buster

9. **Who wrote and recorded Chaka Khan's 'I Feel For You'?**

   a. Marvin Gaye   *b.* Prince   *c.* Lionel Richie

10. **Cliff Richard & The Young Ones had a No. 1 with 'Living Doll', a song originally taken to the top by whom?**

    a. Elvis Presley   *b.* The Beatles   *c.* Cliff Richard

For answers see p311

NO. 1 ALBUMS

1. **Name The Pretenders' only No. 1 album?**

    a. Pretenders   *b. The Great Pretenders*

    c. Pretenders To The Throne

2. ***Tears And Laughter* was a No. 1 album in 1980 by whom?**

    a. Ken Dodd   *b. Don McLean*   *c. Johnny Mathis*

3. **Who were *Back In Black* in 1980?**

    a. Deep Purple   *b. AC/DC*   *c. Johnny Cash*

4. **Complete the title of this Curiosity Killed The Cat album:
   Keep Your _____.**

    a. Love   *b. Money*   *c. Distance*

5. **Who had *Time* at the top in 1981?**

    a. Electric Light Orchestra   *b. Soft Cell*   *c. Godley & Creme*

For answers see p311

6. **Who took us to *New Jersey* in 1988?**

   a. New Order   b. Bon Jovi   c. OMD

7. **Who were *The Visitors* in 1981?**

   a. Adam & The Ants   b. Genesis   c. ABBA

8. **Name Gary Numan's 1980 chart-topper.**

   a. Television   b. Teletubbies   c. Telekon

9. ***Cuts Both Ways* was the title of whose 1989 No. 1?**

   a. The Bangles   b. Gloria Estefan   c. Jason Donovan

10. **How many good reasons did Jason Donovan have in 1989?**

    a. 12   b. 10   c. 6

For answers see p311

1986

1. Which act ended their Top 20 success story with 'New Beginning'?

   a. Phil Fearon   *b.* Spandau Ballet   *c.* Bucks Fizz

2. Which Huey Lewis & The News single made the Top 20 for the second successive year?

   a. 'Do You Believe In Love'

   b. 'The Power Of Love'

   c. 'Stuck With You'

3. What was the name given to the all-star heavy metal charity single ensemble?

   a. Metal Aid   *b.* Rock Aid   *c.* Hear 'n' Aid

4. Complete the title of this Bangles Top 3 hit: 'Walk Like _____'.

   a. A Duck   *b.* A Man   *c.* An Egyptian

5. Elvis Costello married Cait O'Riordan in 1986. What group had she sung with?

   a. Clannad   *b.* The Pogues   *c.* The Belle Stars

For answers see p312

6. **Which *EastEnders* star hit the top with 'Every Loser Wins'?**

   a. Anita Dobson   *b.* Barbara Windsor   *c.* Nick Berry

7. **Which act played to a sell-out crowd at Wembley Stadium for their 'Farewell Concert'?**

   a. The Who   *b.* Wham!   *c.* Madness

8. **Name the singer who published a book this year titled *Is That It*?**

   a. Johnny Rotten   *b.* Bob Geldof   *c.* Elvis Costello

9. **What was the first Top 20 hit for The Communards?**

   a. 'You Are My World'

   b. 'Don't Leave Me This Way'

   c. 'So Cold The Night'

10. **The Beatles returned to the US Top 40 with which old recording?**

    a. 'Love Me Do'   *b.* 'Twist And Shout'   *c.* 'Yesterday'

For answers see p312

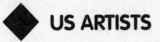

US ARTISTS

1. John Fogerty was the main songwriter in which group?

    a. The Beach Boys   *b.* Jefferson Airplane

    c. Creedence Clearwater Revival

2. Who appeared in the films *The Gambler* and *Coward Of The County*?

    a. Madonna   *b.* Kenny Rogers   *c.* Bob Dylan

3. Which model inspired Billy Joel's hit 'Uptown Girl'?

    a. Christie Brinkley   *b.* Samantha Fox   *c.* Claudia Schiffer

4. John McVie and Mick Fleetwood combined names to form which legendary group?

    a. The Fleetwoods   *b.* Hall & Oates   *c.* Fleetwood Mac

5. What 'cat' provided the middle name for John Mellencamp?

    a. Tiger   *b.* Cougar   *c.* Panther

For answers see p312

6. *Can't Slow Down* was whose most successful album?

a. Lionel Richie   b. Huey Lewis   c. Prince

7. 'Meet Me Half Way' by Kenny Loggins was taken from which film soundtrack?

a. Rocky   b. Ferris Bueller's Day Off   c. Over The Top

8. What was the name of Huey Lewis's backing band?

a. The Information   b. The News   c. The Gossip

9. Who did Bruce Springsteen marry in the mid-'80s?

a. Patti Scialfa   b. Patti Smyth   c. Julianne Phillips

10. What are Simon & Garfunkel's christian names?

a. George & Ringo   b. Paul & Art   c. Michael & Janet

For answers see p312

GUESS THE SONG

1. **Kim Wilde and Bruce Springsteen share which song title?**

   a. 'Kids In America'   *b.* 'Born In The USA'

   c. 'Dancing In The Dark'

2. **Name a-ha's only UK No. 1 single.**

   a. 'Take On Me'

   b. 'The Sun Always Shines On TV'

   c. 'The Living Daylights'

3. **Which James Brown song featured on the *Rocky IV* soundtrack?**

   a. 'Living In America'   *b.* 'I Feel Good'   *c.* 'It's A Man's World'

4. **What was Lionel Richie dancing on in 1986?**

   a. The Table   *b.* The Ceiling   *c.* The Bed

5. **Which James Bond theme song provided a hit for Sheena Easton?**

   a. 'A View To A Kill'

   b. 'For Your Eyes Only'

   c. 'The Living Daylights'

6. **Which George Michael single was banned?**

   a. 'Faith'   *b.* 'Monkey'   *c.* 'I Want Your Sex'

For answers see p312

7. **Name the Olivia Newton-John single that shares its name with an unreleased Stevie Nicks-penned track.**

   a. 'Landslide'

   b. 'The Other Side Of The Mirror'

   c. 'Black Magic Woman'

8. **Which song did Bucks Fizz win the Eurovision Song Contest with?**

   a. 'The Land Of Make Believe'

   b. 'My Camera Never Lies'

   c. 'Making Your Mind Up'

9. **Identify the Loose Ends single that peaked at unlucky No. 13 in 1985.**

   a. 'Hangin' On A String (Contemplating)'

   b. 'Tell Me What You Want'   *c.* 'Nights Of Pleasure'

10. **Which New Order song won a BRIT Award for Best Video in 1988?**

    a. 'True Faith'

    b. 'Touched By The Hand Of God'

    c. 'Bizarre Love Triangle'

For answers see p312

1989 ALBUMS

1. **Name The Bangles' album that their No. 1 'Eternal Flame' was taken from.**

    a. Eternal Flame *b. Everything* *c. Different Light*

2. **Name the album that introduced us to Texas.**

    a. Southside *b. Mother's Heaven* *c. Rick's Road*

3. ***Street Fighting Years* was a No. 1 album for which act?**

    a. The Rolling Stones *b. Simple Minds* *c. Inner City*

4. **Which well-known entertainer had a Top 10 album with *Singalongawaryears*?**

    a. Jimmy Tarbuck *b. Russ Abbot* *c. Max Bygraves*

5. **Which noted artist was also a member of Tin Machine?**

    a. Phil Collins *b. Paul McCartney* *c. David Bowie*

For answers see p313

6. **Which of these albums spent longest at No. 1 in the US this year?**

   a. *Forever Your Girl* – Paula Abdul

   b. *Don't Be Cruel* – Bobby Brown

   c. *Electric Youth* – Debbie Gibson

7. **Lol Tolhurst left which regular albums chart act?**

   a. The Cure   b. The Cult   c. Mike & The Mechanics

8. ***Look Sharp!* was the first of five Top 10 albums by which act?**

   a. Roxette   b. New Kids On The Block   c. Enya

9. **Complete this Simply Red album title: *A New* _____.**

   a. Day   b. Beginning   c. Flame

10. **Who reached No. 1 on the *Road To Hell* this year?**

    a. AC/DC   b. Black Sabbath   c. Chris Rea

For answers see p313

MATCH THE TOP 10 GROUP AND THEIR SINGER

1. Siouxsie & The Banshees
2. The Smiths
3. T'Pau
4. Survivor
5. Splodgenessabounds

6. The Sisters Of Mercy
7. Ten City
8. Texas
9. Transvision Vamp
10. The Undertones

Dave Bickler   Steven Morrissey

Feargal Sharkey   Susan Ballion   Carol Decker

Sharleen Spiteri   Andrew Eldritch   Byron Stingily

Max Splodge   Wendy James

For answers see p313

ZZ TOP

1. 'Gimme All Your _____'

    a. Huggin'   *b.* Kissin'   *c.* Lovin'

2. '_____ Dressed Man'

    a. Sharp   *b.* Nicely   *c.* Smart

3. 'TV _____'

    a. Breakfasts   *b.* Lunches   *c.* Dinners

4. '_____' (part of the body)

    a. Arms   *b.* Legs   *c.* Head

5. '_____ Drinkers'

    a. Beer   *b.* Vodka   *c.* Lager

6. 'I'm Bad, I'm _____

    a. International   *b.* Local   *c.* Nationwide

7. 'Sleeping _____'

    a. Bag   *b.* Rough   *c.* In My Car

8. 'Rough_____'

    a. Boy   *b.* Around The Edges   *c.* Enough

9. '_____ Fly'

    a. Velcro   *b.* The   *c.* Learning To

10. _____ (album)

    a. Before The Fire   *b.* Blaze   *c.* Afterburner

For answers see p313

 **R&B**

1. Name the artist who charted with 'Don't Worry Be Happy'.
   - *a.* Bill Withers
   - *b.* Maxi Priest
   - *c.* Bobby McFerrin

2. Which 'High Energy' act reached the Top 5 in 1984?
   - *a.* Boys Town Gang
   - *b.* The Weather Girls
   - *c.* Evelyn Thomas

3. Who had a hit with 'Don't Push It Don't Force It' in 1980?
   - *a.* The Whispers
   - *b.* Leon Haywood
   - *c.* Stacy Lattisaw

4. 1987 hit act Levert included Sean and Gerald Levert, whose father sang in which R&B act?
   - *a.* The Temptations
   - *b.* The Chi-Lites
   - *c.* The O'Jays

5. Who told us what 'Mama Used To Say'?
   - *a.* Junior Walker
   - *b.* Junior Reid
   - *c.* Junior (aka Norman Giscombe)

For answers see p314

6. **What was the name of the act that showed us 'That's The Way Love Is' in 1989?**

   a. Eight City   *b.* Six City   *c.* Ten City

7. **What was The Four Tops' highest-placed hit of the decade?**

   a. 'Loco In Acapulco'   *b.* 'Don't Walk Away'

   c. 'When She Was My Girl'

8. **Oran 'Juice' Jones had a Top 10 hit in 1986 with which song?**

   a. '(Nothin' Serious) Just Buggin''   *b.* 'The Rain'

   c. 'Love Can't Turn Around'

9. **What was the name of the 'Love Town' hit-maker?**

   a. Mickey Newbury   *b.* Juice Newton

   c. Booker Newberry III

10. **Which duo was 'Solid' in 1985?**

   a. Womack & Womack

   b. Yarbrough & Peoples

   c. Ashford & Simpson

For answers see p314

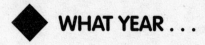
WHAT YEAR . . .

1. . . .was 'Stop The Cavalry' a hit by Jona Lewie?

    a. 1986   *b.* 1983   *c.* 1980

2. . . .was Madonna's hit 'Papa Don't Preach'?

    a. 1984   *b.* 1988   *c.* 1986

3. . . .did Men At Work chart with 'Down Under'?

    a. 1983   *b.* 1985   *c.* 1987

4. . . .was Billy Joel's 'We Didn't Start The Fire'?

    a. 1983   *b.* 1986   *c.* 1989

5. . . .was the Tears For Fears hit 'Everybody Wants To Rule The World'?

    a. 1983   *b.* 1987   *c.* 1985

For answers see p314

6.   . . .did The Pointer Sisters give us a 'Slow Hand'?

   a. 1983   b. 1981   c. 1985

7.   . . .did Liverpool FC score with 'Anfield Rap'?

   a. 1984   b. 1986   c. 1988

8.   . . .was 'Got My Mind Set On You' a No. 2 hit for George Harrison?

   a. 1989   b. 1987   c. 1985

9.   . . .did Musical Youth 'Pass The Dutchie'?

   a. 1986   b. 1984   c. 1982

10.   . . .did Tina Turner's 'What's Love Got To Do With It' chart?

   a. 1981   b. 1984   c. 1987

For answers see p314

1987

1. Which noted female singer won an MTV award for her choreography on a Janet Jackson video?

   a. Toni Basil   *b.* Paula Abdul   *c.* Madonna

2. What was the name of the act that took 'Jive Talkin" back into the Top 10?

   a. Boogie Down Productions

   b. Boogie Box High

   c. Boogie Box

3. Who was named Best British Female Solo Artist at the BRIT awards?

   a. Kim Wilde   *b.* Joan Armatrading   *c.* Kate Bush

4. Actor Bruce Willis hit the Top 10 with the R&B song 'Respect Yourself'. Who originally recorded it?

   a. Aretha Franklin   *b.* Otis Redding   *c.* The Staple Singers

5. Guns N' Roses fulfilled a dream of theirs by playing at which London venue?

   a. London Palladium   *b.* Wembley   *c.* The Marquee Club

For answers see p314

6. **Which popular TV music show ended this year?**

   a. Top Of The Pops   b. The Tube   c. The Word

7. **'No More The Fool' was the last Top 20 single by whom?**

   a. Elkie Brooks   b. Joan Armatrading   c. Sinitta

8. **Who told 'Little Lies' this year?**

   a. Fleetwood Mac   b. Mel & Kim   c. Level 42

9. **Complete this Labi Siffre title: '(Something Inside)**
   _____'.

   a. So Strong   b. Says No   c. Of Me

10. **What act name did Colin Vearncombe use for his hits 'Wonderful Life' and 'Sweetest Smile'?**

   a. Taffy   b. Black   c. The Blow Monkeys

For answers see p314

FILL IN THE GAPS
TRANSPORT

1. 'The _____' (Kylie Minogue)

2. 'Little Red _____' (Prince)

3. 'Frankie' (Sister _____)

4. '_____ Of Love' (The Housemartins)

5. 'Rock The _____' (Forrest)

6. 'Doctorin' The _____' (The Timelords)

7. 'Pink _____' (Natalie Cole)

8. 'Can't Fight This Feeling' (_____)

9. 'Joe Le _____' (Vanessa Paradis)

10. 'Love In An _____' (Aerosmith)

Boat   Cadillac   Caravan   Corvette

Elevator   Loco-Motion   REO Speedwagon   Sledge

Tardis   Taxi

For answers see p315

COMPLETE THE TITLE SINGLES

1. 'Please Don't _____' (KC & The Sunshine Band)

   a. Go   b. Leave   c. Sing

2. 'I'm In The Mood For _____' (The Nolans)

   a. Love   b. Dancing   c. Drinking

3. 'Do The _____' (Coast To Coast)

   a. Hucklebuck   b. Twist   c. Washing

4. 'Green _____' (Shakin' Stevens)

   a. Grass   b. Onions   c. Door

5. 'Don't You Want _____' (The Human League)

   a. It   b. Me   c. Dinner

6. 'Town Called _____' (The Jam)

   a. Malice   b. London   c. Scunthorpe

7. 'You Can't Hurry _____' (Phil Collins)

   a. Up   b. Love   c. Curry

8. 'Rock The _____' (The Clash)

   a. Casbah   b. Boat   c. Cradle

9. 'Girls Just Want To Have _____' (Cyndi Lauper)

   a. Fun   b. Love   c. Clothes

10. 'Break My _____' (Matthew Wilder)

   a. Leg   b. Heart   c. Stride

For answers see p315

1988

1. Who joined Art Of Noise on their hit 'Kiss'?

   a. Prince   *b.* Duane Eddy   *c.* Tom Jones

2. Complete the title of this Danny Wilson hit: '_____ Prayer'.

   a. My   *b.* Your   *c.* Mary's

3. Leslie Wonderman was the real name of which artist?

   a. Taylor Dayne   *b.* Yazz   *c.* Pebbles

4. Whose world tour included seven sell-out dates at Wembley stadium?

   a. Michael Jackson   *b.* Rick Astley   *c.* Bros

5. 'Martha's Harbour' was the only Top 20 entry by which act?

   a. Angry Anderson   *b.* All About Eve   *c.* Breathe

For answers see p315

6. Name the singer voted Best British Male Solo Artist at the BRIT Awards.

  a. Rick Astley *b.* Cliff Richard *c.* George Michael

7. Complete the name of this act: Voice Of The _____.

  a. People *b.* World *c.* Beehive

8. Name the lead singer of Fairground Attraction.

  a. Carol Decker *b.* Eddi Reader *c.* Siobhan Fahey

9. Who starred in the film *Buster*?

  a. Prince *b.* Barbra Streisand *c.* Phil Collins

10. Name Holly Johnson's first solo single.

  a. 'Love Train' *b.* 'Americanos' *c.* 'Atomic City'

For answers see p315

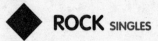 **ROCK** SINGLES

1. Name Freddie Mercury's debut single, a No. 10 hit in 1984.

a. 'The Great Pretender'

b. 'I Was Born To Love You'

c. 'Love Kills'

2. What was Black Sabbath's biggest hit of the '80s?

a. 'Headless Cross'   b. 'Mob Rules'   c. 'Paranoid' (re-issue)

3. What kind of women 'look so cold but feel so warm', according to Iron Maiden?

a. 'Women In Uniform'

b. 'Long-Legged Women'

c. 'Wild Women'

4. What did Van Halen suggest we go ahead and do?

a. 'Jump'   b. 'Walk'   c. 'Make Love'

5. Which member of Led Zeppelin was dealing with a 'Big Log' in 1983?

a. David Gilmour   b. Roger Waters   c. Robert Plant

For answers see p316

6. **The Ramones' one and only Top 10 success came in 1980 with a Ronettes cover. Name the song in question.**

a. 'Be My Baby'   *b.* 'Baby, I Love You'

c. '(The Best Part Of) Breakin' Up'

7. **What was on the loose, according to Thin Lizzy?**

a. Killer   *b.* Moose   *c.* Buffalo

8. **'She's A Little Angel' and 'Don't Waste My Time' were tracks from the *Big Bad* EP. Who released it?**

a. Little Angels   *b.* Saxon   *c.* Queensryche

9. **Which of these Genesis singles is not the title track to a No. 1 album?**

a. 'Abacab'   *b.* 'Invisible Touch'   *c.* 'Mama'

10. **Name the LA band formed in 1983 who have since been 'Around The World' and on a 'Love Rollercoaster'.**

a. Red Hot Chili Peppers   *b.* Nirvana

c. Rage Against The Machine

For answers see p316

GUESS THE ARTIST

1. Who could be described as a 'three-chord boogie band'?

    a. The Cult   *b.* Shalamar   *c.* Status Quo

2. She released two identically titled albums containing her name and an EP with four songs, including 'It's A Mystery' and 'Revelations'. Name her.

    a. Toyah   *b.* Lene Lovich   *c.* Kate Bush

3. Who sang 'I Don't Want To Be A Hero' in 1987?

    a. Tina Turner   *b.* Bonnie Tyler

    c. Clark Datchler (Johnny Hates Jazz)

4. He released the albums *Classics For Dreaming* and *Hansimania* in the early '80s. Who is he?

    a. James Last   *b.* Acker Bilk   *c.* Herb Alpert

5. Which 'lucky' group were voted Best British Newcomers at the BRIT Awards in 1988?

    a. Happy Mondays   *b.* James   *c.* Wet Wet Wet

For answers see p316

6.   **Who was born on 2 December 1981 in Louisiana?**

   a. Britney Spears   *b.* Christina Aguilera   *c.* Jessica Simpson

7.   **This French-Canadian diva won the Eurovision Song Contest in 1988. Who is she?**

   a. Celine Dion   *b.* Jennifer Rush   *c.* Shania Twain

8.   **The 'Nutty Boys' were better known by what name?**

   a. Madness   *b.* The Beat   *c.* The Specials

9.   **Which evergreen singer, who said 'Hello Again' to the charts in 1981, wrote The Monkees' 'I'm A Believer'?**

   a. Tony Christie   *b.* Tom Jones   *c.* Neil Diamond

10. **Who made their chart debut in 1987 with 'Don't Dream It's Over'?**

   a. Split Enz   *b.* Paul Young   *c.* Crowded House

For answers see p316

1989

1. **Which actress/singer got to No. 8 in 1989 with 'Losing My Mind'?**

   a. Barbra Streisand   *b.* Liza Minnelli   *c.* Julie Andrews

2. **The Michael Ball hit 'Love Changes Everything' came from which musical?**

   a. Cats   *b.* Phantom Of The Opera   *c.* Aspects Of Love

3. **What nationality were 'Beds Are Burning' band Midnight Oil?**

   a. American   *b.* Australian   *c.* British

4. **Phil Collins composed 'Two Hearts' with which Motown writer?**

   a. Eddie Holland   *b.* Lamont Dozier   *c.* Norman Whitfield

5. **Craig Logan left which chart-topping act?**

   a. The Beautiful South   *b.* Bros   *c.* Texas

For answers see p316

6. **Which act picked up BRIT Awards for both Best Single and Best Album?**

   a. Phil Collins   b. Annie Lennox   c. Fairground Attraction

7. **Name Shakespears Sister's first hit.**

   a. 'Stay'   b. 'I Don't Care'   c. 'You're History'

8. **ITV's successful TV chart show was called what?**

   a. The Chart Show   b. The Top 20 Show

   c. The Top Records Show

9. **Who recorded the music for the *Batman* movie that came out this year?**

   a. Phil Collins   b. Prince   c. Bruce Springsteen

10. **London's famous Marquee Club celebrated what this year?**

   a. Its 30th birthday   b. Its 25th birthday

   c. Its one millionth customer

For answers see p316

◎ COMPLETE THE NAME OF THE ACT

1. Art Of _____

2. _____ Beyond

3. Black _____

4. _____ Echo

5. All About _____

6. _____ Sound Machine

7. The Four _____

8. Chas & _____

9. _____ Bites

10. Everything But The _____

Tops   Eve   Girl   Dave

It   Brother   Noise   Miami

Pseudo   Box

For answers see p317

ANSWERS

GUESS THE SONG (15–16)

1. *c.* 'True'
2. *b.* 'Cambodia'
3. *c.* 'Soweto'
4. *a.* 'Nobody Told Me'
5. *a.* 'Icing On The Cake'
6. *c.* 'Spread A Little Happiness'
7. *a.* Pandora
8. *b.* 'Happy Birthday'
9. *b.* 'Undercover Of The Night'
10. *a.* A Lover

NO. 1 SINGLES (17–18)

1. *c.* St Winifred's
2. *c.* Philip Bailey
3. *c.* 'I'll Be Missing You' – Puff Daddy
4. *c.* Corner
5. *a.* Lisa Stansfield
6. *b.* Band Aid II
7. *c.* 'Don't Turn Around' – Aswad
8. *b.* 'Belfast Child'
9. *b.* 'Feels Like I'm In Love' – Kelly Marie
10. *c.* Ride

ROCK (ALBUMS) (19–20)

1. *a.* *Wings Of Heaven*
2. *c.* *Midnight*
3. *c.* The Jesus & Mary Chain
4. *c.* Carlos Santana
5. *b.* *Bad For Good*
6. *a.* *Come And Get It*
7. *a.* *Eliminator*
8. *c.* The Offspring
9. *a.* *7800 Fahrenheit*
10. *b.* Visage

◆ ANSWERS

POWER BALLADS (21–22)

1. *b.* Starship
2. *c.* 'Self Control'
3. *b.* Love
4. *c.* John Waite
5. *a.* Robin Beck
6. *a.* 'The Living Years'
7. *a.* Frankie Goes To Hollywood
8. *a.* 1981
9. *b.* Chicago
10. *b.* 'Is This Love'

COMPLETE THE NAME OF THE ACT (23)

1. Coconuts
2. & The Dominos
3. Starr
4. Inner
5. Far
6. Monkeys
7. The Get Fresh Crew
8. Chocolate
9. Camera
10. Modern

1980 (24–25)

1. *b.* 'Call Me'
2. *a.* Olivia Newton-John
3. *c.* The Boomtown Rats
4. *c.* '9 To 5'
5. *c.* One More Time
6. *c.* 'King' / 'Food For Thought'
7. *c.* Stevie Wonder
8. *b.* The Whispers
9. *c.* 'Daytrip To Bangor (Didn't We Have A Lovely Time)'
10. *c.* Whitesnake

ANSWERS

COMPLETE THE NAME OF THE ACT (26)

1. Living
2. Wow
3. Blue
4. Chill
5. Crew
6. News
7. Fiction
8. World
9. KC
10. Mob

MATCH THE TOP 10 GROUP AND THEIR SINGER (27)

1. Noddy Holder
2. Paul Weller
3. Corinne Drewery
4. David Lee Roth
5. Dennis DeYoung
6. Ian Brown
7. Julian Cope
8. Marc Almond
9. Eddie Tenpole
10. Bobby Kimball

SIMPLY RED (28–29)

1. *a.* 'I Won't Feel Bad'
2. *b.* 8 June 1960
3. *b.* 'Money's Too Tight (To Mention)'
4. *a.* No. 51
5. *a.* Hair colour
6. *b.* *Book*
7. *b.* 'Infidelity'
8. *a.* Manchester
9. *a.* *A New Flame*
10. *b.* 60

◆ ANSWERS

POWER BALLADS (30–31)

1. *a.* The Cars
2. *b.* 'Waiting For A Girl Like You'
3. *a.* Alice Cooper
4. *c.* 'Turn Back Time'
5. *b.* Heart
6. *c.* Nick Van Eede
7. *a.* *Star Trek*
8. *a.* 'Listen To Your Heart'
9. *c.* Australia
10. *c.* Africa

SYNTH/ELECTRO (32–33)

1. *a.* Orchestral Manoeuvres In The Dark
2. *c.* Midge Ure
3. *b.* Heaven 17
4. *b.* Alison Moyet
5. *c.* ABC
6. *a.* German
7. *b.* Depeche Mode
8. *c.* Pet Shop Boys
9. *b.* Vince Clarke
10. *a.* *Hysteria*

COVER VERSIONS (34–35)

1. *a.* 'Nothing's Gonna Change My Love For You'
2. *c.* 'Caravan Of Love'
3. *c.* Brian Hyland
4. *b.* Ritchie Valens
5. *b.* Gerry & The Pacemakers
6. *c.* Marvin Gaye
7. *b.* 'Always On My Mind'
8. *c.* The Supremes
9. *b.* 'A Groovy Kind Of Love'
10. *a.* Rosemary Clooney

ANSWERS

ANSWERS

1981 (36–37)

1. *c.* 'Vienna'
2. *c.* The Who
3. *a.* Royal Philharmonic Orchestra
4. *c.* Willcox
5. *c.* Daddy's
6. *b.* Linx
7. *c.* The Four Tops
8. *a.* Tight Fit
9. *a.* Kate Robbins & Beyond
10. *c.* He had died a year earlier

COMPLETE THE TITLE (ALBUMS) (38–39)

1. *a. Beast*
2. *b. Lexicon*
3. *a. Dance*
4. *c. Gap*
5. *a. Pleasure Dome*
6. *b. Jacket*
7. *a. Shop*
8. *a. Reasons*
9. *c. Rattle*
10. *a. USA*

1980 ALBUMS (40–41)

1. *a.* Kate Bush
2. *c.* Motörhead
3. *c.* Billy Joel
4. *b. Signing Off*
5. *b.* Neil Diamond
6. *b.* Adam & The Ants
7. *c.* Yes
8. *b. Super Creeps*
9. *c.* Rush
10. *b.* Genesis

◆ ANSWERS

1. *c.* *Lady Sings The Blues*
2. *b.* Liberian
3. *a.* Diana
4. *a.* Life
5. *a.* Mine
6. *c.* Criminal
7. *c.* Pretty Young Thing
8. *a.* Together
9. *b.* Man
10. *a.* 'One Day In Your Life'

1982 (44–45)

1. *c.* Bow Wow Wow
2. *a.* Bridge
3. *a.* 'Living On The Ceiling'
4. *b.* Bed
5. *c.* Midge Ure
6. *b.* 'Golden Brown'
7. *b.* Christopher Cross
8. *a.* 'Zoom'
9. *c.* Fleetwood Mac
10. *a.* Kid Creole & The Coconuts

FILL IN THE GAPS (PLACES) (46)

1. Lebanon
2. Paris
3. Bangkok
4. Japan
5. China
6. America
7. Hollywood
8. England
9. France
10. Milton Keynes

ANSWERS

1983 (47–48)

1. *b.* 'Sweet Dreams'
2. *c.* Cruel
3. *b.* 'Dear Prudence'
4. *c.* The Jam
5. *a.* 'Buffalo Soldier'
6. *b.* 'Orville's Song'
7. *b.* Their 25th anniversary
8. *c.* Safety
9. *b.* 'Tahiti'
10. *a.* The Assembly

COVER VERSIONS (49–50)

1. *b.* 'Tainted Love'
2. *c.* Frankie Vaughan
3. *b.* 'Love Letters'
4. *c.* Amazulu
5. *b.* Tommy James & The Shondells
6. *c.* 'The Lion Sleeps Tonight'
7. *b.* Eddie Floyd
8. *a.* Millie
9. *b.* 'Cruel Summer'
10. *b.* Smokey Robinson & The Miracles

DANCE (51–52)

1. *c.* Ultravox
2. *b.* 'Love Action (I Believe In Love)'
3. *a.* Three
4. *b.* Depeche Mode
5. *c.* *A Clockwork Orange*
6. *b.* Soft Cell
7. *a.* Martin Fry
8. *b.* 1982
9. *c.* Spandau Ballet
10. *b.* Japan

◆ ANSWERS

1984 (53–54)

1. *c.* Did not make the Top 20
2. *b.* Titles of 1983 films
3. *c.* Alvin Stardust
4. *c.* His hair caught fire
5. *b.* 'Last Christmas' – Wham!
6. *b.* The Firm
7. *b.* (For My Love)
8. *b.* She married Elton John
9. *b.* Moon
10. *c.* Frankie Says. . .

ONE-HIT WONDERS (NAME THE YEAR OF THEIR ONLY TOP 20 HIT) (55)

1. 1983
2. 1985
3. 1981
4. 1988
5. 1984
6. 1980
7. 1989
8. 1987
9. 1982
10. 1986

1981 ALBUMS (56–57)

1. *c.* Cliff Richard
2. *b.* Jon & Vangelis
3. *c.* Elvis Costello
4. *c.* REO Speedwagon
5. *b.* Phil Collins
6. *b.* The Netherlands
7. *b.* Elkie Brooks
8. *b.* Iron Maiden
9. *a.* Glory
10. *c.* Bob Dylan

ANSWERS

1985 (58–59)

1. *c.* Phil Collins
2. *a.* 'Take On Me'
3. *c.* Michael Jackson
4. *b.* Paul Young
5. *c.* Animotion
6. *c.* Carl Perkins
7. *c.* Bruce Springsteen
8. *a.* 'Love Don't Live Here Anymore'
9. *c.* Wham!
10. *c.* Mai Tai

FILL IN THE GAPS (OCCUPATIONS) (60)

1. Mechanics
2. Soldier
3. Baker
4. Police Officer
5. Fisherman
6. Butler
7. Pilot
8. Detective
9. Doctor
10. Maid

COMPLETE THE TITLE (SINGLES) (61)

1. *c.* Beat
2. *b.* Year
3. *c.* 45
4. *b.* Us
5. *c.* Camera
6. *c.* Me
7. *a.* Shadow
8. *c.* Song
9. *c.* Tribes
10. *c.* Doves

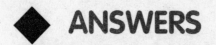

ANSWERS

GIRL POWER (MATCH THE LADIES AND THEIR TOP 10 HITS) (62)

1. 'Circle In The Sand'
2. 'Total Eclipse Of The Heart'
3. 'Knock On Wood'/'Light My Fire'
4. 'I Found Someone'
5. 'Japanese Boy'
6. 'Coming Around Again'
7. 'All Cried Out'
8. 'I Drove All Night'
9. 'I've Never Been To Me'
10. 'Woman In Love'

ORIGINATES FROM (MATCH THE TOP 10 ACT AND THE COUNTRY THEY CAME FROM) (63)

1. Norway
2. Italy
3. USA
4. Germany
5. Jamaica
6. Austria
7. France
8. Australia
9. Switzerland
10. Ireland

ANSWERS

ANSWERS

GUESS THE SONG (64–65)

1. *c.* 'Jackie Wilson Said (I'm In Heaven When You Smile)'
2. *c.* 'Hand In Glove'
3. *a.* 'Say You Really Want Me'
4. *b.* 'A Different Corner'
5. *b.* 'Cha Cha Heels'
6. *b.* 'Push It'
7. *b.* 'The Riddle'
8. *c.* 'A Little Respect'
9. *c.* Arthur Daley
10. *b.* 'Labelled With Love'

1986 (66–67)

1. *c.* No
2. *a.* Double
3. *b.* Cliff Richard
4. *b.* 'New York, New York'
5. *a.* 'The Lady In Red'
6. *b.* Alexander O'Neal
7. *b.* Paul Hardcastle
8. *c.* Tears For Fears
9. *a.* George Benson
10. *a.* 8%

COVER VERSIONS (68–69)

1. *b.* 'Don't Leave Me This Way'
2. *b.* *Carousel*
3. *b.* Quincy Jones
4. *c.* Martha & The Vandellas
5. *a.* The Detroit Spinners
6. *c.* Norman Greenbaum
7. *b.* 1961
8. *c.* Ferry Aid
9. *c.* The Flying Pickets
10. *a.* The Teenagers featuring Frankie Lymon

◆ ANSWERS

MATCH THE TOP 10 GROUP AND THEIR SINGER (70)

1. Andy Partridge
2. Alison Moyet
3. Neil Tennant
4. Gabriele Kerner
5. Chrissie Hynde
6. Helen Folasade Adu
7. Andy McCluskey
8. Jim Kerr
9. Herwig Rüdisser
10. Paddy McAloon

R&B (71–72)

1. b. Midnight Star
2. c. Rufus
3. c. Temptation
4. b. Alyson Williams
5. c. Patti Labelle
6. a. Odyssey
7. a. Keyboards
8. b. Natalie Cole
9. b. Princess
10. c. Rockwell

1987 (73–74)

1. c. 1957
2. b. Anything
3. a. Five Star
4. c. Voice
5. c. Beastie Boys
6. b. Erasure
7. c. Curiosity Killed The Cat
8. b. Pretty
9. b. Alison Moyet
10. a. Steve Winwood

ANSWERS

1982 ALBUMS (75–76)

1. *c.* Asia
2. *c.* League
3. *c.* Men At Work
4. *b.* Thompson Twins
5. *b.* Never charted in the Top 40
6. *b.* Barbra Streisand
7. *a.* Yazoo
8. *b.* The Human League
9. *b.* *Nebraska*
10. *c.* *Kissing*

GIRL POWER (SINGLES) (77–78)

1. *a.* Rochdale
2. *b.* Fern Kinney
3. *b.* Patsy Kensit
4. *b.* Three
5. *b.* Page 3
6. *c.* She's never had a UK No. 1
7. *a.* 'Kitty'
8. *c.* (In the) 'Rush Hour'
9. *a.* Rock lobster
10. *a.* 'My Baby Just Cares For Me'

GENIUS ROUND (79–80)

1. *a.* Aretha Franklin (In chronological order, they are all Elton John's duet partners in the 1980s)
2. *b.* Andy Cox and David Steele
3. *a.* Sun and rain
4. *c.* Elvis Presley
5. *a.* Turkey and Israel
6. *b.* McFly
7. *b.* ABC
8. *a.* 30
9. *b.* 9 (We've Got A Fuzzbox And We're Gonna Use It)
10. *c.* E

◆ ANSWERS

GIRL POWER (ALBUMS) (81–82)

1. c. Never For Ever
2. c. Alison Moyet
3. a. Nelson Mandela 70th Birthday Tribute
4. b. Fajardo
5. a. Deep Sea Skiving
6. a. Cobra
7. a. 1814
8. c. Cher
9. c. Heart
10. a. You Broke My Heart In 17 Places

NOVELTY/ONE-HIT WONDERS (83–84)

1. a. 'Captain Beaky'
2. a. In the kitchen
3. b. Troosers
4. c. Damian
5. a. Suicide
6. a. 'Don't It Make You Feel Good'
7. a. Dancing
8. b. Su Pollard
9. a. Swinger
10. b. 'Eat It'

FILL IN THE GAPS (NUMBERS 1 to 10) (85)

1. 9
2. 3
3. 5
4. 1
5. 2
6. 6
7. 4
8. 7
9. 10
10. 8

ANSWERS

COMPLETE THE TITLE (SINGLES) (86)

1. *b.* Pride
2. *b.* F
3. *a.* System
4. *c.* Manic
5. *b.* Nowhere
6. *a.* Jack
7. *c.* Name
8. *c.* Should
9. *b.* Good
10. *a.* Train

FILL IN THE GAPS (ANIMALS) (87)

1. Elephant
2. Buffalo
3. Frog
4. Dove
5. Horses
6. Snake
7. Housemartins
8. Wolf
9. Rattlesnakes
10. Rats

DUETS (88–89)

1. *c.* Chess
2. *a.* Climie Fisher (Simon Climie)
3. *a.* Renée and Renato
4. *c.* 'Xanadu'
5. *b.* Bill Medley
6. *c.* Andrew Ridgeley
7. *a.* Peter Gabriel and Kate Bush
8. *a.* Dave Stewart
9. *a.* 'Ebony And Ivory' (Paul McCartney and Stevie Wonder)
10. *c.* Sarah Brightman

◆ ANSWERS

1988 (90–91)

1. *b.* 'I Owe You Nothing'
2. *c.* Chubby Checker
3. *b.* The Go-Gos
4. *a.* 'Shake Your Love'
5. *b.* Billy Ocean
6. *c.* The Kinks
7. *b.* Deacon Blue
8. *c.* 'The Loco-Motion'
9. *a.* Transvision Vamp
10. *a.* Michael Jackson

US ARTISTS (SINGLES) (92–93)

1. *b.* John Waite
2. *c.* Tina Turner
3. *b.* Siedah Garrett
4. *a.* Luther Vandross
5. *b.* Van Halen
6. *b.* The Range
7. *b.* 'At This Moment'
8. *a.* Tiffany
9. *c.* Quincy Jones
10. *b.* Guns N' Roses

CHRISTMAS TUNES (94–95)

1. *a.* Wham!'s 'Last Christmas'
2. *c.* Parrot
3. *a.* 'Little Drummer Boy'
4. *c.* Elton John
5. *c.* *The Snowman*
6. *c.* 'When I Fall In Love'
7. *c.* The Flying Pickets' 'Only You'
8. *a.* Santa Claus & The Christmas Trees
9. *a.* Hollis
10. *a.* Bruce Springsteen

ANSWERS

US ARTISTS (ALBUMS) (96–97)

1. *c.* *Footloose*
2. *b.* *Bad*
3. *a.* Stevie Wonder
4. *a.* Bruce Springsteen
5. *c.* *Madonna*
6. *a.* *Attic*
7. *a.* *1984*
8. *c.* Prince
9. *a.* *Beverly Hills Cop*
10. *b.* Journey

1989 (98–99)

1. *c.* Genesis
2. *c.* Paradise
3. *c.* 'Ferry 'Cross The Mersey'
4. *b.* London Boys
5. *b.* Its 25th Birthday
6. *b.* Radio DJs
7. *b.* UB40
8. *c.* Tracy Chapman
9. *a.* 'Stupid Questions'
10. *a.* Bomb The Bass

1983 ALBUMS (100–101)

1. *c.* *The Speed Of Sound*
2. *c.* *Thriller* – Michael Jackson
3. *b.* *True*
4. *b.* *Coda*
5. *b.* Heaven 17
6. *b.* Now That's What I Call Music!
7. *c.* *Cut*
8. *c.* *Dark Side Of The Moon* – Pink Floyd
9. *a.* Big Country
10. *a.* Paul Young

◆ ANSWERS

1980 (102–103)

1. *b.* Jon & Vangelis
2. *c.* Roberta Flack
3. *b.* Mike Berry
4. *a.* Liquid Gold
5. *c.* Martha & The Waves
6. *b.* The Darts
7. *a.* 'Lip Up Fatty'
8. *c.* Affair
9. *b.* 'All Out Of Love'
10. *c.* Black Slate

NO. 1 SINGLES (104–105)

1. *c.* 'Frankie'
2. *a.* Blondie
3. *b.* Geno Washington
4. *a.* *South Pacific*
5. *c.* 'He Ain't Heavy, He's My Brother'
6. *c.* Stuart Goddard
7. *c.* Renée
8. *b.* Bob Geldof
9. *a.* PhD
10. *a.* 'I Just Called To Say I Love You'

MATCH THE GROUPS AND THEIR TOP 10 HITS (106)

1. 'Wishful Thinking'
2. 'Drama!'
3. 'Never Never'
4. 'Wishing (If I Had A Photograph Of You)'
5. 'Hard Habit To Break'
6. 'Election Day'
7. 'Alone'
8. 'Love Me Do'
9. 'It Started With A Kiss'
10. 'Song For Whoever'

ANSWERS

ROCK (SINGLES) (107–108)

1. *c.* The Skids
2. *a.* 'All Night Long'
3. *b.* Steel
4. *a.* 'Poison'
5. *a.* 'Patience'
6. *c.* The Law
7. *a.* Beds
8. *b.* BB King
9. *a.* 'Love Missile F1-11'
10. *a.* Sugar

1981 (109–110)

1. *c.* Godley & Creme
2. *c.* Bill Wyman
3. *c.* Graham Bonnet
4. *a.* Lunatics
5. *c.* 'Happy Birthday'
6. *b.* '(Do) The Hucklebuck'
7. *b.* Earth, Wind & Fire
8. *a.* Freeez
9. *b.* Tom Tom Club
10. *a.* Landscape

MATCH THE GROUP MEMBER WITH THEIR GROUP (111)

1. Status Quo
2. Sky
3. Pat & Mick
4. New Edition
5. New Kids On The Block
6. S'Express
7. Shakatak
8. Run-DMC
9. Pepsi & Shirlie
10. Squeeze

◆ ANSWERS

FILL IN THE GAPS (FRUIT AND VEG) (112)

1. Berry
2. Apple
3. Banana
4. Orange
5. Grape
6. Bean
7. Coconut
8. Cherry
9. Onion
10. Root

MATCH THE GROUP MEMBER WITH THEIR GROUP (113)

1. UB40
2. The Real Thing
3. The Nolans
4. Ollie & Jerry
5. Queen
6. Salt-n-Pepa
7. Shakespears Sister
8. Spandau Ballet
9. Wham!
10. The Weather Girls

GUESS THE SONG (114–115)

1. *a.* Pencil case
2. *a.* 'Girl You Know It's True'
3. *a.* 'On The Beach'
4. *b.* 'Rio'
5. *b.* Rose
6. *a.* '68 Guns'
7. *a.* 'Da Da Da'
8. *c.* My Roots
9. *b.* 'Never Gonna Give You Up'
10. *b.* 'Trouble'

ANSWERS

MATCH THE GROUPS AND THEIR TOP 10 HITS (116)

1. 'Can't Shake The Feeling'
2. 'Nightshift'
3. 'Poison Arrow'
4. 'I Need You'
5. 'Can I Play With Madness'
6. 'Special Brew'
7. 'Human'
8. 'Ant Rap'
9. 'We Close Our Eyes'
10. 'Blind Vision'

1982 (117–118)

1. *b.* Seven
2. *b.* Hot Chocolate
3. *c.* 'Young Guns (Go For It)'
4. *a.* XTC
5. *a.* Foster & Allen
6. *c.* Marvin Gaye
7. *b.* 'Maid Of Orleans (The Waltz Joan Of Arc)'
8. *c.* 'Precious'
9. *a.* Cher
10. *c.* Ozzy Osbourne

THE CLASH (119)

1. *a.* Bank
2. *a.* Call
3. *a.* UK
4. *c.* Seven
5. *c.* Stay / Go
6. *b.* England
7. *c.* Kingston
8. *b.* Law
9. *a.* Star
10. *a.* Hell

◆ ANSWERS

GIRL POWER (SINGLES) (120–121)

1. *c.* 'Martha's Harbour'
2. *c.* Martha Wash
3. *a.* Paul Weller
4. *c.* *Bread*
5. *a.* Dionne Warwick
6. *b.* Lionel Richie
7. *a.* Pointer
8. *a.* Al Green
9. *a.* 'Eighth Day'
10. *a.* 'Breakfast In Bed'

U2 (122)

1. *b.* Town
2. *a.* *October*
3. *c.* Pride
4. *a.* *America*
5. *a.* You
6. *c.* Harlem
7. *a.* Joshua
8. *b.* God's
9. *c.* As One
10. *b.* *Blood Red*

FILL IN THE GAPS (DAYS AND MONTHS) (123)

1. February
2. Friday
3. December
4. Sunday
5. Saturday
6. Tuesday
7. May
8. Wednesday
9. April
10. September

ANSWERS

GIRL POWER (SINGLES) (124–125)

1. *c.* 'Atomic'
2. *a.* Japan
3. *c.* On a flight from the US to Switzerland
4. *b.* Belinda Carlisle
5. *c.* *Neighbours*
6. *b.* Kelly Marie
7. *b.* 'Lucky Star' (1984)
8. *a.* Summer Olympic Games in Seoul, 1988
9. *c.* Eddi Reader
10. *b.* Orinoco

1984 ALBUMS (126–127)

1. *a.* The Style Council
2. *b.* *Purple Rain – Prince*
3. *c.* *Legend – The Best Of Bob Marley & The Wailers*
4. *b.* Alison Moyet
5. *a.* *Diamond Life*
6. *a.* Culture Club
7. *b.* The Pointer Sisters
8. *c.* *Consent*
9. *b.* Stevie Wonder
10. *b.* Queen

FILL IN THE GAPS (THE FAMILY) (128)

1. Sister
2. Father
3. Brother
4. Mother
5. Daddy
6. Uncle
7. Son
8. Daughter
9. Grandma
10. Grandpa

◆ ANSWERS

ANSWERS

1983 (129–130)

1. *a.* 'Candy Girl'
2. *b.* By The Pool
3. *c.* Young
4. *c.* 'Just Got Lucky'
5. *c.* Imposter
6. *a.* Altered Images
7. *b.* The Maisonettes
8. *c.* Toto
9. *b.* The Funk Masters
10. *b.* Limahl

NO. 1 ALBUMS (131–132)

1. *b.* *Double Fantasy*
2. *a.* Johnny Hates Jazz
3. *c.* Kate Bush
4. *b.* *The First Album*
5. *b.* Marvin Lee Aday
6. *c.* Work
7. *a.* 3
8. *a.* Rose Royce
9. *b.* Tina Turner
10. *c.* *Association*

DUETS (133–134)

1. *c.* 'Don't Leave Me This Way'
2. *b.* James Ingram
3. *b.* Hank B. Marvin
4. *b.* Melle Mel
5. *a.* Got married
6. *a.* 'What Have I Done To Deserve This?'
7. *b.* 1985
8. *b.* 'Islands In The Stream'
9. *a.* 21 years
10. *a.* Glenn Hoddle and Chris Waddle

ANSWERS

BUCKS FIZZ (135)

1. *b.* Making / Mind
2. *a.* Action
3. *b.* Nights
4. *c.* Camera
5. *c.* *Ready*
6. *a.* Heat
7. *b.* London
8. *a.* Talking
9. *c.* Heart / Blue
10. *b.* Mamba Seyra

DUETS (136–137)

1. *a.* Willie Nelson
2. *a.* Barbara Dickson
3. *a.* Aretha Franklin
4. *b.* Steve Harley
5. *a.* Marilyn Martin
6. *b.* Bryan Adams
7. *b.* Michael Jackson
8. *b.* In Electric Dreams
9. *b.* Captain & Tennille
10. *b.* 'Cha Cha Heels'

GIRL POWER (MATCH THE LADIES AND THEIR TOP 10 HITS) (138)

1. 'French Kissin' In The USA'
2. 'My Toot Toot'
3. 'This Time I Know It's For Real'
4. 'Foolish Beat'
5. 'High Energy'
6. 'Let's Hear It For The Boy'
7. 'All The Love In The World'
8. 'No More The Fool'
9. 'Upside Down'
10. 'See The Day'

ANSWERS

ORIGINATES FROM (MATCH THE TOP 10 ACT AND THE COUNTRY THEY CAME FROM) (139)

1. Spain
2. Australia
3. UK
4. US
5. Guyana
6. Sweden
7. Austria
8. Germany
9. Greece
10. France

1984 (140–141)

1. *a.* 'Smalltown Boy'
2. *b.* Altered Images
3. *b.* Gloria Estefan
4. *b.* The Colourfield
5. *c.* Matthew Wilder
6. *c.* Neil Kinnock
7. *a.* Lionel Richie
8. *c.* Victory
9. *b.* Traffic
10. *c.* In Central Park, New York

FILL IN THE GAPS (GIRLS' NAMES) (142)

1. Julie
2. Isla
3. Charlotte
4. Sara
5. Eileen
6. Maggie
7. Jane
8. Caroline
9. Tracie
10. Carrie

ANSWERS

MATCH THE GROUP MEMBER WITH THEIR GROUP (143)

1. Rainbow
2. The Specials
3. The Ramones
4. The Proclaimers
5. Shalamar
6. The Rah Band
7. Soul II Soul
8. Thompson Twins
9. Roxette
10. Sister Sledge

CHRISTMAS TUNES (144–145)

1. *b.* 1984
2. *a.* 'Merry Christmas Everyone'
3. *a.* Dawn Ralph
4. *a.* No. 2
5. *c.* 'Mistletoe And Wine'
6. *b.* Chris Rea
7. *a.* 'Merry Xmas Everybody'
8. *c.* Spaceman
9. *a.* Wrapping
10. *a.* '2000 Miles'

1985 (146–147)

1. *b.* Mick Jones
2. *a.* (Man In Motion)
3. *b.* Bonnie Tyler
4. *c.* *Desperately Seeking Susan*
5. *b.* Billy Idol
6. *c.* Jesus
7. *b.* Daryl Hall
8. *c.* Billy Joel
9. *b.* The Far Corporation
10. *c.* Dire Straits

◆ ANSWERS

POWER BALLADS (148–149)

1. *a.* Cinderella
2. *c.* Ontario, Canada
3. *b.* Jennifer Warnes
4. *c.* Thorn
5. *a.* 'Need You Tonight'
6. *a.* Love
7. *b.* *The Joshua Tree*
8. *a.* 'Feel Like'
9. *a.* Steve Winwood
10. *a.* Bon Jovi

US ARTISTS (SINGLES) (150–151)

1. *c.* Whitney Houston
2. *b.* Roy Orbison
3. *a.* *Back To The Future*
4. *b.* Cyndi Lauper
5. *a.* *Cocktail*
6. *a.* *New Jersey*
7. *a.* 1982
8. *b.* *III*
9. *b.* Tone Loc
10. *a.* *Best Shots*

FILL IN THE GAPS (THE WEATHER) (152)

1. Rain
2. Air
3. Sun
4. Summer
5. Chill
6. Rainbow
7. Lightning
8. Winter
9. Wind
10. Storm

ANSWERS

1985 ALBUMS (153–154)

1. *c.* Meat Loaf
2. *c.* Prince
3. *c.* *Arms*
4. *b.* Mick Jagger
5. *b.* *Little Creatures*
6. *c.* Kate Bush
7. *a.* *No Jacket Required*
8. *c.* Tears For Fears
9. *a.* *Drum*
10. *c.* *Bat Out Of Hell* – Meat Loaf

GIRL POWER (MATCH THE LADIES AND THEIR TOP 10 HITS) (155)

1. 'Together We Are Beautiful'
2. 'Searchin' (I Gotta Find A Man)'
3. 'Let's Wait Awhile'
4. 'Will You'
5. 'Come Into My Life'
6. 'Don't Wanna Lose You'
7. 'Can't Be With You Tonight'
8. 'Fame'
9. 'Set Me Free'
10. 'Ain't Nothin' Goin' On But The Rent'

MATCH THE GROUP MEMBER WITH THEIR GROUP (156)

1. Tears For Fears
2. Visage
3. The Stray Cats
4. The Who
5. The Tourists
6. Ultravox
7. Was (Not Was)
8. Thin Lizzy
9. Talking Heads
10. The Stranglers

◆ ANSWERS

ROCK (SINGLES) (157–158)

1. *c.* Megadeth
2. *a.* 'Is There Anybody There?' / 'Another Piece Of Meat'
3. *a.* 'We've Got Tonite'
4. *b.* Coat
5. *a.* Sweden
6. *a.* Joe Perry and Steven Tyler
7. *a.* Steve
8. *c.* $5.98
9. *c.* Deep Purple
10. *c.* Derek & The Dominos

1986 (159–160)

1. *b.* Modern Talking
2. *c.* Bob Geldof
3. *b.* Cutting Crew
4. *a.* PIL
5. *a.* 'Sometimes'
6. *c.* *Sid And Nancy*
7. *c.* America
8. *a.* 'Eloise'
9. *c.* Thompson Twins
10. *c.* Five Star

FILL IN THE GAPS (THE BODY) (161)

1. Heart
2. Arm
3. Legs
4. Hand
5. Head
6. Foot
7. Eye
8. Elbow
9. Finger
10. Mouth

ANSWERS

GUESS THE ARTIST (162–163)

1. *a.* Elvis Presley
2. *b.* Mary Sandeman
3. *b.* Talking Heads
4. *b.* The Kids From 'Fame'
5. *a.* Natalie Cole
6. *c.* Wendy Fraser
7. *c.* Brennan
8. *b.* Pink Floyd
9. *c.* Kenny Rogers
10. *a.* The Stone Roses

NO. 1 SINGLES (164–165)

1. *a.* 'Oh Julie' – Shakin' Stevens
2. *b.* The Damned
3. *c.* The Right Stuff
4. *b.* 'Super Trouper'
5. *a.* 'Dreams Of Children'
6. *c.* 'I Should Be So Lucky'
7. *c.* The Timelords
8. *a.* 'Goody Two Shoes'
9. *b.* Music Theatre
10. *c.* 3

NEW ORDER (166–167)

1. *b.* Gillian Gilbert
2. *b.* 12-inch
3. *a.* 'Ceremony'
4. *c.* Manchester
5. *a.* *Power, Corruption And Lies*
6. *c.* Peter Hook
7. *a.* Johnny Marr
8. *a.* John Peel
9. *b.* *Technique*
10. *a.* Green

◆ ANSWERS

GIRL POWER (168–169)

1. *a.* Me
2. *a.* Usher
3. *a.* 79
4. *b.* Germany
5. *b.* 'Ain't Nobody'
6. *a.* Helen Folasade Adu, Nigeria
7. *b.* 'Move Closer'
8. *b.* Caron Wheeler
9. *a.* Legs & Co.
10. *b.* A woman

1987 (170–171)

1. *c.* America
2. *c.* The Smiths
3. *a.* Rikki
4. *c.* Jan Hammer
5. *c.* Siedah Garrett
6. *a.* 'Animal'
7. *b.* Bananarama
8. *c.* Peter Gabriel
9. *b.* Bonita
10. *a.* George Harrison

NO. 1 SINGLES (172–173)

1. *c.* 'Reet Petite (The Sweetest Girl In Town)' – Jackie Wilson
2. *c.* 'Into The Groove'
3. *b.* John Lennon
4. *a.* 'The Lion Sleeps Tonight' – Tight Fit
5. *c.* Diana Ross
6. *a.* 'You Spin Me Round (Like A Record)'
7. *b.* Stevie Wonder
8. *b.* Leslie Charles
9. *c.* Nothing
10. *c.* The Plastic Population

ANSWERS

ADAM & THE ANTS (174)

1. *a.* Dog
2. *c.* Parisians
3. *a.* Frontier
4. *a.* Stand
5. *c.* Charming
6. *a.* Deutscher
7. *a.* Puss 'n
8. *b.* 9
9. *a.* Rap
10. *c.* Sox

LYRICS (175–176)

1. *b.* Roses
2. *c.* Barbara
3. *c.* The middle
4. *a.* His heart
5. *c.* Jitterbug
6. *b.* Reality
7. *c.* Dynasty
8. *a.* Miami To Canada
9. *c.* Caligula
10. *b.* The church

1988 (177–178)

1. *b.* Prince
2. *b.* Pebbles
3. *b.* 'Suedehead'
4. *c.* 'That's The Way It Is'
5. *a.* Joe Brown
6. *c.* Brother Beyond
7. *b.* Tiffany
8. *a.* Pete Waterman
9. *c.* Status Quo
10. *b.* Sonny Bono

◆ ANSWERS

1986 ALBUMS (179–180)

1. *b.* Barbara Dickson
2. *a.* *Slippery When Wet*
3. *c.* Whitney Houston
4. *c.* Paul Simon
5. *b.* *True Blue*
6. *b.* Larry Blackmon
7. *b.* Dire Straits
8. *c.* INXS
9. *b.* *Steel*
10. *a.* Bryan Ferry & Roxy Music

MATCH THE GROUPS AND THEIR TOP 10 HITS (181)

1. 'Wedding Bells'
2. 'Big In Japan'
3. 'It Doesn't Have To Be This Way'
4. 'I Could Be Happy'
5. 'The Love Cats'
6. 'Can't Get Used To Losing You'
7. 'O L'Amour'
8. 'One Step Further'
9. 'I'm Not Scared'
10. 'Too Much'

TV & FILM (182–183)

1. *a.* Billy Connolly
2. *c.* Jan Hammer
3. *c.* Christopher Cross
4. *c.* *Blue Peter*
5. *c.* *Batman*
6. *b.* Bobby Brown
7. *c.* Gladys Knight
8. *b.* *Buster*
9. *c.* 'Suddenly'
10. *b.* Irene Cara

ANSWERS

US ARTISTS (SINGLES) (184–185)

1. *b.* Daryl & John
2. *a.* Fleetwood Mac
3. *c.* Bette Davis
4. *a.* Sheena Easton
5. *b.* The Bangles
6. *c.* Mr Mister
7. *c.* Blondie
8. *c.* Joseph
9. *a.* The Commodores
10. *c.* Cyndi Lauper

1989 (186–187)

1. *b.* Mick Fleetwood
2. *c.* Boy Meets Girl
3. *b.* La Na Nee Nee Noo Noo
4. *b.* The Bangles
5. *b.* Aitken
6. *b.* Tina Turner
7. *b.* 'How Long' – Ace
8. *b.* Roxette
9. *c.* 'Pacific'
10. *b.* It was his 100th single

MADNESS (188)

1. *b.* Cairo
2. *c.* Trousers
3. *a.* Seven
4. *c.* Grey
5. *a.* Car
6. *c.* Madness
7. *b.* Dove
8. *c.* Pronounce
9. *c.* Michael Caine
10. *c.* Sweetest

◆ ANSWERS

GIRL POWER (MATCH THE LADIES AND THEIR TOP 10 HITS) (189)

1. 'Feels Like I'm In Love'
2. 'Gloria'
3. 'Four Letter Word'
4. 'O Superman'
5. 'More Than In Love'
6. 'Babooshka'
7. 'Got To Be Certain'
8. 'All Around The World'
9. 'A New England'
10. 'Dress You Up'

NO. 1 SINGLES (190–191)

1. b. Jive Bunny
2. b. Partners In Kryme
3. c. Berlin
4. b. 'Now Those Days Are Gone'
5. c. '19'
6. c. Nicole
7. b. Ashes To Ashes
8. c. 'Baby Jane'
9. b. Dexy's Midnight Runners
10. c. 'You Win Again'

DANCE (192–193)

1. c. Jackmaster
2. b. The Hues Corporation
3. c. Phil Fearon & Galaxy
4. a. 'Male Stripper'
5. b. Gregory Abbott
6. b. Elisa Fiorillo
7. a. Krush
8. a. French
9. a. Soul II Soul
10. c. Madonna

ANSWERS

NON-HUMAN (194–195)

1. *b.* Casserole your gran
2. *b.* 'Swing The Mood'
3. *c.* Sheep
4. *a.* 'Rabbit'
5. *c.* Green
6. *b.* Kitchen
7. *a.* Snowmen
8. *b.* Fish
9. *c.* Frogs
10. *c.* The Tweets

DANCE (196–197)

1. *b.* 'Funky Town'
2. *c.* D Mob
3. *a.* 'Street Dance'
4. *a.* Imagination
5. *b.* Boys Town Gang
6. *b.* Shannon
7. *c.* Brixton
8. *b.* Colonel Abrams
9. *a.* 'Walking On Sunshine'
10. *a.* Kaoma

1980 (198–199)

1. *b.* 'Runaway Boys'
2. *c.* The Crusaders
3. *b.* 'Eighth Day'
4. *b.* George Benson
5. *b.* Minder
6. *b.* The Ramones
7. *a.* 'Sexy Eyes'
8. *a.* 'Computer Game'
9. *b.* Ottawan
10. *c.* Brothers Johnson

◆ ANSWERS

ROCK (ALBUMS) (200–201)

1. *a.* John Cougar
2. *b.* Iron Maiden
3. *b.* Black Sabbath
4. *b.* Roxy Music
5. *c.* Toto
6. *b.* Fleetwood Mac
7. *b.* Nylon
8. *c.* *The Gift*
9. *a.* Trevor Horn
10. *c.* *Permanent Vacation*

COMPLETE THE TITLE (SINGLES) (202)

1. *b.* Hero
2. *b.* Street
3. *c.* Spirit
4. *c.* Red
5. *b.* Boardwalk
6. *c.* Volume
7. *b.* Around
8. *b.* Dis
9. *b.* Mistletoe
10. *a.* Love

FILL IN THE GAPS (FAMOUS PEOPLE / NAMES) (203)

1. Buddy Holly
2. Tarzan
3. Robert De Niro
4. Michael Caine
5. Aretha Franklin
6. Billie Jean
7. John Kettley
8. Don Quixote
9. Nelson Mandela
10. Flintstone

ANSWERS

ANSWERS

STATUS QUO (204)

1. *b.* *12*
2. *b.* Proposing
3. *b.* Drive My Car
4. *a.* John
5. *c.* Wanderer
6. *b.* Red
7. *b.* Running
8. *a.* Blues
9. *c.* Blues
10. *b.* The Love

1987 ALBUMS (205–206)

1. *c.* Wet Wet Wet
2. *c.* *Tango*
3. *b.* Depeche Mode
4. *a.* *Dirty Dancing* (soundtrack)
5. *c.* *Brothers In Arms* – Dire Straits
6. *c.* Swing Out Sister
7. *c.* *The Joshua Tree*
8. *b.* Alexander O'Neal
9. *a.* Howard Jones
10. *b.* *City Of Light*

1981 (207–208)

1. *b.* 'In The Air Tonight'
2. *b.* *Cats*
3. *b.* Claws
4. *c.* Kim Wilde
5. *c.* Racey
6. *c.* Was a No. 1
7. *c.* Diana Ross
8. *c.* (Boy Meets Girl)
9. *c.* 'Over The Rainbow – You Belong To Me'
10. *b.* Jackie DeShannon

◆ ANSWERS

NOVELTY/ONE-HIT WONDERS (209–210)

1. *b.* Harry Enfield
2. *b.* Baltimora
3. *b.* The Sweet People
4. *b.* Black Lace
5. *c.* 'Stars On The Beatles'
6. *c.* Nana Mouskouri
7. *c.* Power
8. *c.* Bing Crosby
9. *b.* Spagna
10. *a.* Denise LaSalle

1982 (211–212)

1. *b.* Putting Out Fire
2. *c.* Nicole
3. *c.* Blackhearts
4. *c.* Adrian Gurvitz
5. *b.* Bananarama
6. *b.* England World Cup Squad
7. *c.* The Kids From Fame
8. *c.* The Gibb Brothers
9. *c.* A Miracle
10. *a.* Scotland

PET SHOP BOYS (213)

1. *a.* Girls
2. *b.* Love
3. *c.* Money
4. *b.* This
5. *b.* Always
6. *a.* Domino
7. *c.* Devices
8. *a.* Alright
9. *a.* Divided by
10. *c.* King's Cross

ANSWERS

ANSWERS

FILL IN THE GAPS (COLOURS) (214)

1. Red
2. Grey
3. Green
4. Yellow
5. Blue
6. White
7. Orange
8. Purple
9. Black
10. Pink

1983 (215–216)

1. *a.* 'Hand In Glove'
2. *c.* Big Country
3. *b.* (Living It Up)
4. *b.* Sweet Dreams
5. *b.* Maggie Reilly
6. *b.* Fun Boy Three
7. *a.* Dead Or Alive
8. *a.* 'Ooh To Be Ah'
9. *c.* The World's Famous Supreme Team
10. *b.* Marilyn

ROCK (ALBUMS) (217–218)

1. *a.* *The House Of Blue Light*
2. *b.* Ian
3. *c.* Alice Cooper
4. *a.* Samson
5. *b.* *Kick*
6. *a.* *The Jimi Hendrix Concerts*
7. *c.* Chicks
8. *a.* The Moody Blues
9. *c.* Sheffield
10. *b.* *Green*

◆ ANSWERS

FILL IN THE GAPS (NUMBERS – ALBUMS) (219)

1. 7
2. 17
3. 85
4. 4
5. 3
6. 8
7. 100
8. 45
9. 10,000
10. 101

1988 ALBUMS (220–221)

1. *b.* Marillion
2. *c.* Jazz
3. *b.* The Housemartins
4. *b.* Was No. 1 for 12 weeks
5. *a.* Terence Trent D'Arby
6. *c.* Your Video
7. *a.* Steve Winwood
8. *c.* Guns N' Roses
9. *c.* Nothing
10. *c.* Nothing Like The Sun – Sting

1984 (222–223)

1. *b.* Council Collective
2. *a.* 'Love Resurrection'
3. *c.* Mick Jagger
4. *b.* Laura Branigan
5. *c.* Street
6. *b.* Michael Jackson
7. *b.* Alphaville
8. *c.* Slim Jim Phantom
9. *a.* 'Nelson Mandela'
10. *a.* Cliff Richard

ANSWERS

1. 'Mama'
2. 'Party Fears Two'
3. 'Rise To The Occasion'
4. 'You Win Again'
5. 'Cry Wolf'
6. 'Lean On Me'
7. 'Big Fun'
8. 'Somewhere In My Heart'
9. 'Chance'
10. 'One Of Us'

1. Phil Fearon
2. Johnny Rotten
3. Marti Pellow
4. Sting
5. Green Gartside
6. Bryan Ferry
7. Kevin Cronin
8. David Coverdale
9. Martin Degville
10. Mick Hucknall

1985 (226–227)

1. *b.* Arcadia
2. *b.* 'Ben'
3. *b.* Vikki
4. *a.* Wham!
5. *c.* 'Saving All My Love For You'
6. *c.* Did not reach the Top 40
7. *b.* Bruce Springsteen
8. *b.* Sonny & Cher
9. *b.* George Michael
10. *b.* Nowhere

◆ ANSWERS

GUESS THE ARTIST (228–229)

1. c. Bob Dylan
2. a. Mike Oldfield
3. a. The Damned
4. a. Echo & The Bunnymen
5. a. Yes
6. b. Neil Young
7. b. AC/DC
8. a. Grandmaster Flash
9. b. a-ha
10. c. Paul Weller

WHAT YEAR . . . (230–231)

1. b. 1985
2. c. 1989
3. c. 1987
4. c. 1989
5. b. 1984
6. b. 1981
7. b. 1986
8. a. 1984
9. b. 1981
10. b. 1987

NO. 1 SINGLES (232–233)

1. a. 1961
2. b. Gaynor Hopkins
3. c. Attraction
4. c. Gene Pitney
5. c. Appleby
6. b. Boris Gardiner
7. b. Europe
8. c. 'Too Much Too Young'
9. c. 'Fame'
10. c. Barry & Robin Gibb

ANSWERS

TV & FILM (234–235)

1. *b.* Natalie Cole
2. *a.* *Glass*
3. *a.* Jarreau
4. *b.* *Gun*
5. *c.* Su Pollard
6. *b.* Paul McCartney
7. *c.* 'Donald Where's Your Troosers'
8. *a.* Coca-Cola
9. *c.* 'Love Letters'
10. *a.* Survivor

COVER VERSIONS (236–237)

1. *b.* Ken Boothe
2. *c.* Lion
3. *c.* Neil Diamond
4. *c.* The Damned
5. *c.* Los Lobos
6. *b.* Prince
7. *c.* Rod Stewart
8. *a.* The Paragons
9. *b.* Prince
10. *c.* Cliff Richard

NO. 1 ALBUMS (238–239)

1. *a.* *Pretenders*
2. *c.* Johnny Mathis
3. *b.* AC/DC
4. *c.* *Distance*
5. *a.* Electric Light Orchestra
6. *b.* Bon Jovi
7. *c.* ABBA
8. *c.* Telekon
9. *b.* Gloria Estefan
10. *b.* 10

◆ ANSWERS

1986 (240–241)

1. *c.* Bucks Fizz
2. *b.* 'The Power Of Love'
3. *c.* Hear 'n' Aid
4. *c.* An Egyptian
5. *b.* The Pogues
6. *c.* Nick Berry
7. *b.* Wham!
8. *b.* Bob Geldof
9. *b.* 'Don't Leave Me This Way'
10. *b.* 'Twist And Shout'

US ARTISTS (242–243)

1. *c.* Creedence Clearwater Revival
2. *b.* Kenny Rogers
3. *a.* Christie Brinkley
4. *c.* Fleetwood Mac
5. *b.* Cougar
6. *a.* Lionel Richie
7. *c.* *Over The Top*
8. *b.* The News
9. *c.* Julianne Phillips
10. *b.* Paul & Art

GUESS THE SONG (244–245)

1. *c.* 'Dancing In The Dark'
2. *b.* 'The Sun Always Shines On TV'
3. *a.* 'Living In America'
4. *b.* The Ceiling
5. *b.* 'For Your Eyes Only'
6. *c.* 'I Want Your Sex'
7. *a.* 'Landslide'
8. *c.* 'Making Your Mind Up'
9. *a.* 'Hangin' On A String-(Contemplating)'
10. *a.* 'True Faith'

ANSWERS

1989 ALBUMS (246–247)

1. b. *Everything*
2. a. *Southside*
3. b. Simple Minds
4. c. Max Bygraves
5. c. David Bowie
6. a. *Forever Your Girl* – Paula Abdul
7. a. The Cure
8. a. Roxette
9. c. *Flame*
10. c. Chris Rea

MATCH THE TOP 10 GROUP AND THEIR SINGER (248)

1. Susan Ballion
2. Steven Morrissey
3. Carol Decker
4. Dave Bickler
5. Max Splodge
6. Andrew Eldritch
7. Byron Stingily
8. Sharleen Spiteri
9. Wendy James
10. Feargal Sharkey

ZZ TOP (249)

1. c. Lovin'
2. a. Sharp
3. c. Dinners
4. b. Legs
5. a. Beer
6. c. Nationwide
7. a. Bag
8. a. Boy
9. a. Velcro
10. c. *Afterburner*

◆ ANSWERS

R&B (250–251)

1. *c.* Bobby McFerrin
2. *c.* Evelyn Thomas
3. *b.* Leon Haywood
4. *c.* The O'Jays
5. *c.* Junior (aka Norman Giscombe)
6. *c.* Ten City
7. *c.* 'When She Was My Girl'
8. *b.* 'The Rain'
9. *c.* Booker Newberry III
10. *c.* Ashford & Simpson

WHAT YEAR . . . (252–253)

1. *c.* 1980
2. *c.* 1986
3. *a.* 1983
4. *c.* 1989
5. *c.* 1985
6. *b.* 1981
7. *c.* 1988
8. *b.* 1987
9. *c.* 1982
10. *b.* 1984

1987 (254–255)

1. *b.* Paula Abdul
2. *b.* Boogie Box High
3. *c.* Kate Bush
4. *c.* The Staple Singers
5. *c.* The Marquee Club
6. *b.* *The Tube*
7. *a.* Elkie Brooks
8. *a.* Fleetwood Mac
9. *a.* So Strong
10. *b.* Black

ANSWERS

ANSWERS

FILL IN THE GAPS (TRANSPORT) (256)

1. Loco-Motion
2. Corvette
3. Sledge
4. Caravan
5. Boat
6. Tardis
7. Cadillac
8. REO Speedwagon
9. Taxi
10. Elevator

COMPLETE THE TITLE (SINGLES) (257)

1. *a.* Go
2. *b.* Dancing
3. *a.* Hucklebuck
4. *c.* Door
5. *b.* Me
6. *a.* Malice
7. *b.* Love
8. *b.* Boat
9. *a.* Fun
10. *c.* Stride

1988 (258–259)

1. *c.* Tom Jones
2. *c.* Mary's
3. *a.* Taylor Dayne
4. *a.* Michael Jackson
5. *b.* All About Eve
6. *c.* George Michael
7. *c.* Beehive
8. *b.* Eddi Reader
9. *c.* Phil Collins
10. *a.* 'Love Train'

◆ ANSWERS

ROCK (SINGLES) (260–261)

1. *c.* 'Love Kills'
2. *c.* 'Paranoid' (re-issue)
3. *a.* 'Women In Uniform'
4. *a.* 'Jump'
5. *c.* Robert Plant
6. *b.* 'Baby, I Love You'
7. *a.* Killer
8. *a.* Little Angels
9. *c.* 'Mama'
10. *a.* Red Hot Chili Peppers

GUESS THE ARTIST (262–263)

1. *c.* Status Quo
2. *a.* Toyah
3. *c.* Clark Datchler (Johnny Hates Jazz)
4. *a.* James Last
5. *c.* Wet Wet Wet
6. *a.* Britney Spears
7. *a.* Celine Dion
8. *a.* Madness
9. *c.* Neil Diamond
10. *c.* Crowded House

1989 (264–265)

1. *b.* Liza Minnelli
2. *c.* *Aspects Of Love*
3. *b.* Australian
4. *b.* Lamont Dozier
5. *b.* Bros
6. *c.* Fairground Attraction
7. *c.* 'You're History'
8. *a.* *The Chart Show*
9. *b.* Prince
10. *a.* Its 30th birthday

ANSWERS

COMPLETE THE NAME OF THE ACT (266)

1. Noise
2. Brother
3. Box
4. Pseudo
5. Eve
6. Miami
7. Tops
8. Dave
9. It
10. Girl

ACKNOWLEDGEMENTS

With thanks to Dave McAleer, Matt White, Mike Lynch, Justin Lewis, Darren Haynes and Colin Hughes.